JESSICA'S PEOPLE

We wandered idly along the lane with its neatly trimmed hedges on each side, my friend Pat and me. We had spent the afternoon playing with the kittens, now we were hungry and I hoped mum would be in a better mood. She had snapped at us this morning when I had brought home one of the kittens, a little ginger one—she yelled at me to take it back, saying we already have a cat.

As we came through the kitchen door a lovely smell greeted us. Mam was making blackcurrant jam. She smiled at us now, as she placed the big pan of jam on a cold slab to cool before she poured it into the jars all washed and ready.

We watched as she cut off two huge slices of soda bread, spread them thickly with butter and then jam from a saucer which had cooled on the table.

We sat on the doorstep and munched contentedly. Pat said, I wish my Mammy could make jam like this. Can't she then? I asked. Naw, she tried it once, it was rhubarb I think, it was all green and runny. Daddy wouldn't try it, he said it looked like cat's pee.

I saw Mam turn away and smile, but Auntie Jeannie, who was sitting knitting, said, You shouldn't let her play with that boy, she is rude enough already.

Mother didn't answer, she put the frying pan on and sliced cold potatoes and thick slices of bacon. My three brothers and sister would be back from school soon.

Cover photograph of Jessie, aged about 5

The cresses on the water and the sorrels are at hand,
And the cuckoo calling daily his note of mimic bland,
And the bold thrush sings so bravely his song in the forest grand
On the fair hills of holy Ireland.

WB Yeats

JESSICA'S

PEOPLE

———

Jessie Woodger

JESSICA'S PEOPLE
First published 1998

Typeset and published by John Owen Smith
12 Hillside Close, Headley Down, Hampshire GU35 8BL
Tel/Fax: 01428 712892
E-mail: wordsmith@headley1.demon.co.uk

ISBN 1-873855-25-7

Printed and bound by Antony Rowe Ltd, Bumper's Farm, Chippenham, Wiltshire

With grateful thanks to Joyce Stevens for reading my first badly punctuated manuscript, to Janet Woodger for her advice and encouragement, and to Jo Smith for finally sorting out the muddle.

Jessie Woodger, Headley 1998

Descendants of Jack SCARLETT

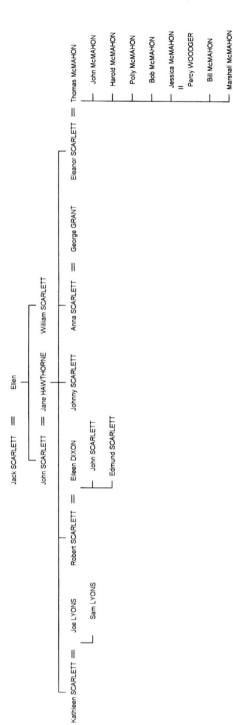

Contents

Fermanagh Gates   9
The Scarlett Roses   61
Jessica   133
And now …   163

Fermanagh Gates

∽∂∽∂∽∂

There is not in the wide world a valley so sweet
As that vale in whose bosom the bright waters meet.
Oh the last rays of feeling and life must depart
Ere the bloom of that valley shall fade from my heart.

Thomas Moore

Fermanagh Gates

1870

The Castle Sanderson estate lay partly in Cavan and partly in Fermanagh. There were three avenues leading to the Castle with imposing high white iron gates and spiked railings each side: the Belturbet gates so called because they lead off the road to Belturbet, a nice little town on the river Erne; the Sweep gates, I suppose because the road there swept round a double bend; and lastly the Fermanagh gates, which were the ones used mostly by the gentry in their fine carriages. Here there was a pretty little gate lodge and a bridge, and the avenue led past the little estate church with its surrounding grave yard in which lay the bodies of the Sanderson family for over 200 years, in a crypt with an iron gate and a strong metal door.

A few minutes' walk from the castle was a beautiful wild garden. It had been started by one of the Sanderson ladies many years before, and each lady in turn had added her own touches to it. The result was lovely—many beautiful trees had been brought back from all over the world, azaleas scented the air and lily of the valley added their fragrance. Streams with wooden bridges over them ran into a little lake with an island, where wild fowl nested in peace from predators. Such a peaceful place, even the bees, drunk on nectar, moved slowly from flower to flower.

Colonel Sanderson was a bustling, bad tempered little man and most of his staff feared him. His wife was an invalid in a wheelchair—she was a kind, gentle lady, and was the only one who didn't fear the Colonel. He could never outwit her in any argument—she just laughed at him.

The little road ran gently down. It was narrow and stony, and the carriage tracks were filled occasionally with rough stones from the

11

quarry. On one side was the long stone wall behind which was the Castle Sanderson estate, on the other side were fields belonging to small farms. A fine farmhouse stood back from the road, belonging to the Scarlett family and now owned by William Scarlett, who lived with his widowed mother Ellen.

His father, Jack Scarlett, had met an untimely end. One day he had gone into the bull pen, as he did every day to clean it out, and began to work with a fork in his hand. Suddenly, the bull moved towards him and knocked him against an oak post. The attack was so sudden and unexpected that he dropped the fork, but the bull kept pushing him against the post. He shouted and William came running, managing to get the bull away by hooking the ring in its nose to the chain on the fence, but Jack's legs wouldn't move.

William dragged his screaming father out and shut the gate, then Jack passed out with agony, and Ellen and William laid him on an old door and carried him into the house. The doctor came and said he thought his back was broken. Several more doctors were brought in, but Jack remained numb from the waist down. He lived on, and a bed was put in the dining room. He hated it there, so William called in a mason to build a bedroom with a French door so Jack could see out, and a washroom behind the bedroom.

Jack had another son called John, who was apprenticed to a cabinet maker. He had made a will leaving the farm to William, but decided to give John £200 and half an acre of ground when he was eighteen. He told him to build a house on it, but John didn't see what he needed a house for—he lived at home and walked each day over to work in Sam Smiley's workshop.

Jack explained to him that when he and Ellen died, William would marry and have a family—then John would need a house to have a home of his own.

John saw the sense of it, but did not think much about it until in church one Sunday he saw the most beautiful girl he had ever seen. She was visiting some relations in the neighbourhood, and after the service John cleverly got an introduction to her. Her name was Jane Hawthorne, a farmer's daughter, and it was love at first sight. John visited her during her stay, and found that she lived about 15 miles away.

So he found an architect who planned the house as John wanted it, and a mason started to build it. John worked at it too, when he found the time. It had a sitting room and large kitchen, a scullery and a dining room downstairs—Jane said she didn't need a dining-room but they had it—three bedrooms upstairs and a loft with a floor ceiling and a skylight. It took nearly two years to finish it. By this time John had proposed to Jane, asked her father for her hand and had the blessing of both families. They had a lovely wedding, and moved into the new house. John had made a lot of the furniture, Jane the curtains, her mother had given them a beautiful patchwork quilt, and Ellen some bed linen and table-cloths. Other relations had given them crockery, pots and pans—Jane arranged it all, and she and John were very happy.

They had their first child, a little girl named Kathleen, and 18 months after that she had Robert. But Jack Scarlett had caught a chest infection and eventually died a month after Kathleen was born, and though Jane tried to help Ellen, two small children took up a lot of her time.

Old Sam Smiley wasn't well either. John loved his work there—the feel of the wood: oak, walnut, mahogany, he loved them all—and Sam had made him a partner and put Smiley & Scarlett on the gate. They'd always had plenty of work, and when Sam was ill, they took on a young lad to learn the trade. Sam had been complaining of chest pains for a while, and one day John came into the workshop and found him slumped over the bench. He helped him into bed and got the doctor, but Sam died quietly in the night. Sam had a brother who'd gone to America years before, and had died there. When the solicitor, Mr Lawson, arrived at the house and read the will, he had left everything to John, who he said had been like a son.

Ellen Scarlett was sixty-two and beginning to feel her age. She worked hard and was often weary. She wished she'd had a daughter—Jane was a lovely daughter-in-law, but her children kept her busy.

One day as she sat by her window, she saw a shabby-looking man walk slowly up to the door. At the gate she could see what seemed to be a donkey and cart with a woman sitting in it.

"I'm sorry to trouble you," he said, "but my wife isn't well—could we have a little water?"

Ellen looked at his pinched white face and shabby jacket. "Bring her in and I'll make a cup of tea," she replied, "I was just about to make one."

The two came in—Jane made them sit down, put a big mug in their hands and handed round slices of bread and jam. The young woman was pale and fair-haired, with dark circles round her eyes. "I

13

haven't had a cup of tea for weeks," she said, and they ate quickly as though they were afraid someone would take the food away.

William came in at that moment. "Where are you going?" he said. The man explained that he had been a ploughman on an estate in Roscommon, but the gentleman had sold off all the stock and put a caretaker in. They had got notice to leave the cottage and had been turned out four weeks ago. All their belongings were on the cart—they had been travelling around, sleeping under the cart, and couldn't find any work. They'd had a baby boy, but he had died a fortnight ago—a priest had given him a Christian burial. Mary was still mourning for the baby, he said. His name was Terry Donaghue and Mary was his wife.

William could see that Ellen's heart ached for them, and called her into the sitting room. "I'm going over to John's" he said. "Sam's cottage is empty—if he lets them live there, I could use Terry if he's a ploughman."

Ellen asked them to stay for the evening meal and showed Terry where to put the donkey to graze. William came back with John and Jane and the two children. John agreed with William—he badly needed help and so did Ellen—and Terry could work, and Mary too when she was stronger.

The meal was two thick rashers of bacon each, cabbage, and potatoes boiled in their jackets. The Donaghues couldn't believe their luck—they didn't know what to say, just nodded 'yes' to everything. William told them that they could have two pints of milk each day and as many potatoes as they needed, the cottage was free, and he would pay Terry a wage of 7/6d per week.

Mary went into raptures when she saw the cottage—the big oak dresser filled with plates, the wide fire place with pot hooks and crane, a bed in each room, lovely warm feather beds. Jane had taken the blankets and sheets home and washed them. They found peat and wood in the shed and lit the fire. Ellen and Jane had left a basket packed with bread, butter, jam, tea and sugar and a can of milk. Mary and Terry washed themselves and fell into bed—the first comfortable sleep they had had in weeks, and the best bed ever.

Next morning very early, they slipped over to the catholic church and thanked God for his goodness—the old priest found them kneeling together and they told him the whole story—he blessed them and they went back to begin a new life.

It was a wise decision taking on the Donaghue's. Mary came in and helped Terry with the milking, and she knew how to churn and bake. She washed and ironed till Ellen had to beg her to stop. Terry was the same—he knew how to make thorn hedging and he managed the horses with kindness, and both were as honest as the day was long. Ellen became very thin—she had a nagging pain in her side. William called the doctor and he gave her something for the pain. She finally took to her bed two years after the Donaghue's had come, and died in her sleep one night.

• • •

1902

The Scarlett family were sitting around the table for their evening meal. John Scarlett, a big man with a full black beard and soft brown eyes, looked around the table at this family.

His wife Jane, calm, capable, the darling of his life. He thanked God for her every day. On her right sat Robert, 16 years old, quiet, intelligent and hard-working. John was a cabinet maker and Robert was learning the trade with him. On his left was Johnny. Johnny was 14 years old, a restless boy always looking for something different to do; a bit unstable, John thought, but perhaps he will settle. Next was Kathleen—she was 17½, a rather plain girl, but very capable—then Anna, 12 years old, demure, her dark hair parted in the middle and in two plaits, her pale skin perfect and her enormous hazel eyes always cast down, with a rather prissy little mouth below a rather large nose which just stopped her from being beautiful. By his side was his youngest daughter Eleanor, a little dark-haired girl, full of life and full of love. She's like quicksilver, he thought fondly.

Kathleen brought a large casserole and placed it in front of him, Anna brought in a pile of warm plates, and Jane carried a dish of floury boiled potatoes and a dish of cabbage.

Everyone sat with arms folded and waited for John to say grace, "Thank you God for this good food which you have provided for us; may we all be truly thankful, amen."

John ladled out a portion for each one, with a dumpling as light as a feather, and all started to eat. "Well Johnny," he asked, "how was your day at school?"

"It was alright Sir, thank you, but Master Lyons gave Joe ten of the best. He made him drop his trousers in front of the whole class."

"What on earth had he done to deserve that?" asked Jane.

"He only got 8 marks out of 10 for geography, and 9 out of 10 for history."

15

"But that wasn't a bad mark was it?"

"No," said Johnny, "but Joe gets the same every day for something."

"Well," commented Jane, "it seems to me a very harsh way to treat his eldest son. Joe isn't as bright as William and the girls, but he isn't stupid either."

When the meal was over the girls cleared away the dishes and washed up. Eleanor, only eight years old, wiped the table and put the vase of flowers in the middle. John and Jane settled on each side of the huge range. Robert disappeared upstairs and could be heard practising his violin, and Johnny got out his homework on the table.

John sat thinking about little Joe Lyons. He wondered why his father, James Lyons, was so hard on the boy. He seemed a nice lad; very civil and good mannered when spoken to, and John had often seen him at work in the garden, sometimes with his mother Margaret, but often quite alone.

• • •

In the flat under the school rooms Barbara Brown was wondering the same thing. She was the other teacher in the little country school; she taught the six to eleven year olds and Master James Lyons taught the eleven to fourteens. Because she lived alone, with little to spend her time at, she took home all the homework, James' as well as her own. When the school day ended that Friday afternoon, James had come through from his class room and she'd looked at him with her clear blue eyes and said, "I don't understand why you caned Joe. I gave him his marks because I thought his work was quite good, well above average."

He turned to her, eyes blazing. "Quite good! Quite good is not good enough from my children. I expect and demand excellence from my family. Joe is lazy—he doesn't use his brain."

"Perhaps his brain is not as good as yours or his brother and sister's," said Barbara.

"Everyone has brains. I will beat him until he uses them," he roared.

"Maybe you will kill him first," retorted Miss Brown.

He glared at her and went out, banging the door.

Barbara Brown looked worried. Why did he pick on Joe? Did he resent Joe's relationship with his mother? Barbara had often seen them engrossed in the garden, talking and discussing what was best where, and she remembered hearing of James' little fling fifteen years

16

ago with Margaret, the daughter of a well-to-do owner of several shops. The fling ended in a rather hurried wedding. Perhaps James hadn't wanted marriage. It seemed that Joe was the direct cause of James' obvious unhappiness. She didn't know what to think. James could be violent, and she had heard that at weekends he drove his horse and trap into Clones, the nearest town, and came home only because the horse knew the way, James sitting, drunk and sleeping, the whole seven miles. She had also heard that he visited a lively widow in town who lost her wealthy husband through a heart attack. She had been living a very gay life ever since. But Barbara had heard only rumours—she never repeated what she had heard, after all she had to work with the man.

Master Lyons left the school and walked quickly across the playground to his home. The four children were around the table at home work, and Margaret was preparing vegetables for the evening meal. James spoke to no-one and went through to the sitting room where he slumped into his chair. Presently he went upstairs, shaved, changed his clothes and came downstairs to where the table was now laid for the evening meal.

The children sat down in their places. James turned to Joe, who was looking uncomfortable. "Catch Prince and harness him," he said.

"Now Sir?" said Joe.

"Of course now," he shouted.

Margaret put the food on the table, James said grace and Margaret dished up two dinners, put lids on them and put them into the oven. James smiled grimly, "I see you are not eating with us my dear wife."

"No," she said "I'll eat with Joe later. You are going out?"

"I am."

"Might one ask where?"

"You may ask, but I won't tell you," he answered.

They all ate in silence, then James got up and went out. Joe stood at the horse's head, fondling the dark velvet nose. James took the reins from him, jumped into the trap, he gave the horse a sharp flick with the whip and they were gone.

Joe came into the house, washed his hands, and his mother put his plate in front of him.

"How's your bottom, Joe?" she asked.

"Sore," he replied.

"I will look at it in a minute."

"No, it will be alright" Joe said.

After the meal was cleared, Margaret tided up the kitchen. Joe had fallen asleep in the armchair. Her heart melted looking at him, his auburn hair slightly curled and his beautiful eyelashes resting on his freckled cheeks. She checked the oil lamp and sat down, while Joe slept on. William tiptoed into the kitchen and looked at this brother. "Da really hurt him today," he said, "and he never cried, not once." Then suddenly, "I hate my father, I hate, hate, hate him."

"Hush, son, don't hate him. Pity him—he is a very unhappy man."

"Why is he unhappy? He has you, and us, and his work. We are not short of money, are we Mam?"

"No, son, we are not short of money," she said. "Your father has great ability. He shouldn't be here in this backwater—he is capable of teaching in a more advanced learning establishment."

"Well, why doesn't he," William cried.

"He has tried several times," his mother said, "but I don't know why he doesn't get the jobs. Perhaps he interviews badly, or perhaps his strong personality comes out, I don't know."

"Perhaps his violent nature comes through," William said.

"Go to bed William," his mother said, "Joe will have to see to the horses when he comes back.."

She glanced at the clock—9 o'clock—James wouldn't be home for several hours yet. Last time he came home drunk he had dragged Joe out of his bed to see to the horse—he might as well sleep where he was, poor love.

Margaret herself was dozing when she heard the clatter of hooves in the yard. She looked at the clock—10.15—James was early. She lit the hurricane lamp and called Joe.

"Your father is home—see to the horse, there's a good boy, and be careful."

Joe rubbed his eyes, took the lamp from his mother and went out. It was raining heavily as he crossed the yard. His father was sitting in the trap, but Joe looked in horror at the horse; covered in suds, his sides going in and out like a bellows and his breath rasping.

James fumbled with the door, opened it, missed the step and fell down. "Well, help me up, damn you," he shouted.

Joe took hold of his father's arm, his mind still on the horse. Somehow as he stood up, his father's fist caught him in the mouth, and he stumbled across to the back door. His head reeling, Joe started to take off the harness—Prince was still gasping. As he took the saddle off he ran his hand over the horse's rump, and could feel the ridges where the lash had landed time after time all the way home. He fetched the water bucket. Prince dropped his nose but didn't drink— his back legs seemed to be buckling under him.

"Oh, God, Prince," the boy sobbed, "don't lie down—I won't be able to get you back on your feet."

But Prince was kneeling now, and slowly toppled over on to his side. The painful breathing still went on. Joe rubbed him with handfuls of hay, but he died with Joe hugging his head and sobbing.

James in the meantime had stumbled through the kitchen into the hall and up the stairs where he collapsed on the bed fully clothed.

Margaret waited until all was quiet, then put a shawl round her shoulders and crossed the yard. She screamed as she saw her son, blood pouring from his mouth and nose, kneeling beside the lovely old horse.

"Come in Joe," she pleaded, "come in and get warm."

"Never," he sobbed. "Never will I enter that house again as long as I live."

"Joe, son, you are only fourteen. Where will you go and where will you stay?" she asked.

Joe stood up and said, "I will go to the Scarletts now, and in the morning I will decide."

He touched his mother's cheek and walked out into the rain. She watched him until he was out of sight, then turned slowly and went indoors, she made up the fire and settled in her chair for the night, crying bitterly.

Joe walked as fast as he could. Sometimes he had to sit down as dizziness overcame him; his head ached and his wet trousers were rubbing against the weals on his bottom. At midnight he reached the Scarlett's house. It was in darkness. He knocked loudly on the door, then again, and John Scarlett appeared, having pulled on his trousers in a hurry.

"My God, Joe, what has happened?" He looked at the young boy, his face streaked with blood, but Joe had reached the end of his tether and passed out on the doorstep. John picked him up and carried him to the fire, still burning low, then called to Jane.

"Fetch the bath, John," she said when Joe at last opened his eyes. She undressed him and helped him into the bath in front of the fire, looking in horror at the big bruise between his shoulder blades and the weals on his buttocks, now rubbed raw by the wet tweed trousers. He was blue with cold and his teeth chattered as he tried to tell them what had happened. They dried him gently. Jane fetched a healing ointment and put it on his buttocks, then she dressed him in a warm night shirt of Johnny's, put him on the couch and piled rugs and blankets around him.

"I'll stay with him—you go to bed John"

John shook his head "I'll stay too—he doesn't look too good."

At five o'clock Jane touched Joe's forehead and he was very hot. She sponged him and changed his night shirt but he became restless, muttering to himself and crying. At six o'clock John harnessed his horse and went to fetch the doctor, who sensed the urgency and came back with him.

"He has pneumonia," he said. "I will make up some medicine for him—you must keep him sponged and I think you should fetch his parents."

John nodded grimly. He would have a word with James Lyons!

At that moment James Lyons was waking up with a roaring headache. He had made a fool of himself. When he left the house the previous evening he'd called into a pub on the way and bought a bottle of whisky and a bottle of gin and presented himself at Widow Houston's door. She'd opened the door looking very smart.

"Why James," she said, "I didn't expect you tonight, but come in."

He found another woman and two men there, sitting around the table playing cards, a small pile of coins in front of each. Bridie Houston introduced them, and one of the men said, "Do you play pontoon, James?"

"I know the game," James said. "I'll have a hand with you."

He won the first two hands, but then the stakes went higher and he started losing, and the more he lost the oftener he replenished his glass. Finally at 9.30, all his money was gone and the whisky bottle was empty. He said goodnight as civilly as he could and left.

Sitting on the side of his bed he looked at his dirty trousers and he could smell his sweat. He felt a mess. He could still hear the derisive laughter of Bridie and her friends as she saw him to the door. He washed his face and changed his clothes, his head ached and his hands were shaking. He heard the front door knocker and heard Margaret going up the hall. A man's voice—that sounds like John Scarlett—what on earth does he want on a Saturday morning? He heard them walk down the hall and into the kitchen, and the murmur of voices.

James came down and into the kitchen. "Good morning, John," he said.

"It is not a good morning," said John. "It is a very bad morning for us all. Your son Joe is in my home seriously ill and your horse is lying dead in your yard. Mrs Lyons is coming back with me now, and you had better tidy up the loose ends here—and perhaps you can explain it all to your other children. Joe needs his mother."

With that, John took Margaret out and helped her into the trap—and soon she was looking down at her sick boy.

Kathleen had lit a fire in the dining-room and Robert had helped Jane to carry Joe in to where she had made up the day bed. He was hot and restless and muttering to himself. Jane had changed the sheets yet again, and Kathleen was sponging his face and hands.

"His temperature is still very high," Jane said, "but we are doing all we can."

"Oh, Jane," Margaret said, the tears streaming down her face, "if it wasn't for you and your good family he would probably be dead—how can I ever thank you?"

"Don't bother about all that—right now he needs you. Try to keep him cool, and just hold him and talk to him. With God's help and our prayers he will recover."

Little Eleanor crept into the room, and put her arms around Margaret. "Mrs Lyons, I have been praying very hard for Joe, I know he will be alright."

"Thank you Eleanor, you are a good child. I am sure you prayers will be heard!"

For three days Joe lay between life and death. John had brought in two easy chairs and Jane and Margaret worked together, having a short sleep sometimes, but on Monday evening at last Joe cooled down and fell into a peaceful sleep.

The doctor had been in and out all the time, and on Sunday afternoon James and William came. James looking ashamed and worried—if Joe knew he was there he showed no sign, but John called James into the sitting room, and there he found the doctor and Reverend Conway. James knew he was in trouble.

"James Lyons, I am horrified at what I've heard," the Reverend said. "I don't think you are a fit person to be in charge of the children in my parish. You have killed your horse and perhaps your son. So what do you think is going to happen to you? I would sack you here and now, but I am thinking of your wife and family. If you ever lift a cane to any child again I will have no alternative."

James left the room then and went home. His two daughters, Selina and Hannah, though still at school had cooked a dinner of sorts and kept the house tidy. They looked at him and saw how distressed he was, but they were too frightened to speak. They had never been beaten by him, but they knew about his terrible temper.

On Monday night Margaret came home. Joe was able to sit up, Jane had made him beef tea and he had enjoyed it. He told his mother he wouldn't be home, and John and Jane had assured her that he would be welcome to stay until he was fit again.

Three days later the doctor let him get up and sit in a chair, and Jane found him reading a gardening book. She smiled at him. "There are a lot of more interesting books in here Joe."

"I love this one," he replied, "there's a lot to learn in here."

His recovery was a slow one. He still had nightmares about poor dead Prince, and even in his waking hours he went through the scene again and again. He didn't want to see his father. He could only feel disgust that anyone could hurt Prince—always so obedient and willing, he never needed a whip—a "Gee-up boy" sent him flying happily along. His own injuries he simply forgot about.

He didn't know what he would do when he was recovered. At the moment he had very little energy and hardly any appetite, but he received a lot of attention at the Scarlett's. Kathleen fussed over him and tried everything to make him eat. She made delicious concoctions which he tried to eat just to please her. He still coughed—the Doctor said it was good for him to clear his chest—and Jane made honey and lemon with a taste of brandy which she gave him at night. At least he was beginning to sleep better.

One Sunday, Eleanor was looking out of the window and suddenly whooped for joy. She ran down to the gate crying, "Thomas, how lovely of you to come and see me."

The tall boy smiled down at her, "I've come to see Joe, and you," he said.

She hugged his arm. "Look, Mammy," she said, "Thomas has come to see Joe and Me."

Jane smiled at Thomas. "I don't know what I'm going to do with this child," she said, "she is very bold."

"But Mammy, Thomas was my very best friend at school. He carried my bag home every day. Now he has left school, I have to carry it myself."

"How is work going, Thomas?" Jane asked.

"I like it," he replied, "sometimes it's a bit hard, but this week Jim and I have been working in the wild garden. It is really beautiful."

"What do you do in there?" Jane asked.

"Well, we're not allowed to prune or cut back anything—we just pull out a few weeds and sweep the paths. We've planted 50 shrubs—they have a name I can't pronounce—we planted them on the castle side of the lake. Madam came down in her wheelchair and watched us; she said there will be colour most of the year. She is a very clever lady and knows all the names of the trees and plants."

Jane felt a bit sorry for Thomas McMahon. He'd had to leave school at 12 years old because his family needed his wages. He was a tall strong young man, and Eleanor worshipped him.

He went though to the sitting room where Joe was, and they sat and talked. Johnny came in too, and he was a great story teller. Jane could hear them laughing: it would do Joe good having his friends around him. His mother came often, but she fussed him and worried about him, and Jane thought he was always a little worse after she left.

Week by week Joe improved, and a bed was brought over from John's brother's farm and put up in the loft where Robert and Johnny slept. The three boys got on well, and many a night John had to call up for a bit of quiet!

Jane and John went over to the farm often. William, John's brother, lived there alone since the mother died. The couple called Terry and Mary Donaghue came in every day and milked, and Mary did the house work and cooking while Terry worked outside.

William had had a cough for a long time, and he often looked tired. John wished he had married, but he never seemed to bother with girls—he was now 44 and still managed alone.

One Sunday, John and Jane found him looking very pale. Mary Donaghue was there, and when she went into the kitchen Jane followed her.

"I was just coming to see you," Mary said. "I noticed William has been spitting blood, when I washed his handkerchiefs. I thought you ought to know."

"Has he been to the doctor?" Jane asked.

"Yes, he went on Friday—but he didn't tell me what the doctor said. I didn't like to ask him, but I have been worried about him, and Terry says he has no strength at all and sits down every few minutes."

Meanwhile John and William had been talking, and William told him that the doctor thought he had TB.

23

John was horrified. "Well, will you go into hospital," he said.

"No," William said, "it is too late for that. I wondered what Johnny was going to do when he quits school. He is 14 now isn't he? If he could come over and help Terry, I'd feel a lot better."

"Of course he can come," John said, "and Kathleen too, if you need her. I know Mary is great in the house, but she has a home of her own to run as well."

So Johnny went and lived in the farm. Kathleen came over every day, and as William got worse the whole family spent time there. John was heartbroken—he loved his elder brother, and had never envied him for getting the family home. He had grown up there and knew how to do most things, but his woodwork was his livelihood as well as his hobby.

In September, William asked John to get his solicitor to come and see him. He said he had things to sort out. A time was arranged and William asked the doctor and rector to come on the same day.

The solicitor took a pile of papers which William kept in a drawer and spent a lot of time studying them. At last he said, "William, you are a wealthy man."

William looked up in surprise "Am I?"

"My friend, you haven't opened a bank statement in years."

"Well, I wasn't spending. When I found too much money in the drawer, I banked it. My needs are few—we live off the land here."

"Well there seems to be at least £10,000 in the bank, you have a well stocked farm, a good house—yes William, I would say you are wealthy."

William gave the solicitor a list of things that he wanted done, and he wrote it out. Mary looked in to say that the doctor and the Reverend Conway were here. They witnessed the will and left. William felt happier and at peace with himself. The Reverend Conway had given him holy communion and promised to come back soon—he felt at ease and somehow cleansed.

A week later he died.

When the solicitor read the will, he had left £500 to Mary and Terry, £100 each to Johnny and Kathleen, £500 to the church, and the farm and the rest of the money to John.

John was staggered at the amount. He'd guessed that there had been money in the bank in his father's time, but so much?

Now there was the problem of owning two houses, both large and in good repair, and a cottage. He and Jane talked about it late into the night.

At last Jane said, "I'll go over every day and keep things running. I don't know if Mary and Terry will stay now they have a bit of money, but if they do I will just keep an eye on things." Then she added, "But what about Johnny? He is young to stay there on his own. We ought to bring him home to sleep I think."

But Johnny wanted to stay at the farm. He liked doing what he wanted in the evenings. Mary and Terry agreed to stay for the present and sit on their money. Terry said he would try and buy a few acres with a house, but he wanted to look around first: "No hurry," he said.

Johnny used to walk through the house when he was alone. There was a picture over the fireplace in the dinning room, and he remembered the Reverend Conway looking at it and saying to William: "I think it is a Stubbs." William said his father had bought it at an auction about 20 years ago—he thought it a good picture of a horse,.

Johnny also thought it was good, and was clever enough to guess that it was valuable. How much it was worth he had no idea, but he meant to find out.

So he slept on at the farm, and he began to go out at night to some friends he had made, and they played cards.

John had decided to give Johnny a small wage, and Jane bought the groceries and Mary cooked for him, as she had done for William. John also doubled Terry's wages, as he was now in charge of the farm. But Terry was uneasy with Johnny—he was quite a good worker, but sneaked off sometimes and didn't seem to take a great interest in the farm at all. Johnny mentioned one day that he would like to harness William's horse and take him for a drive.

"You had better ask your father," said Terry. "That horse hasn't been in harness for several months now, and he was always very lively."

"I could handle him," Johnny said, "father taught me and Robert to drive."

"Well, you ask him," Terry replied.

One night after Terry and Mary had gone home, Johnny was alone. He hadn't any money left and it was no good going over to O'Reilly's without it. He went into the dining room and looked at the picture—he felt the surface—it was canvas. Then lifting it down—it was quite heavy—he wrapped it in a sack and hid it in his room.

He got up early the next morning, harnessed the horse, and put the picture under the seat. Mary and Terry were milking, and he left a note saying he would be back at dinner time, and it was alright with his

25

father to drive the horse—then he started off for Cavan, a town about 10 miles away. He knew there was an antique dealer there—he had passed the shop before and seen pictures in the window.

He tied the horse outside and carried the picture in. An elderly man met him, and he told him he wanted to sell the picture. The man looked intently at it and turned it over. "Where did you get this?" he asked.

"My uncle died a couple of months back," Johnny said, "and he left it to me in his will."

The man looked out and saw the fine horse and trap outside—it all sounded genuine enough.

"What are you asking for it?"

"Twenty-five pounds," said Johnny.

"I will give you twenty," said the man. "I'm not a rich man—I may have trouble selling it."

So Johnny took the £20 and went home.

When he was eating his dinner, Mary said, "I was dusting the dining room today—that picture is gone—did your mother take it?"

"Oh, I forgot to tell you," Johnny said, "I heard this crash after I went to bed—I came down to see what it was—the picture had fallen down on that big brass fender—it was in bits."

"What did you do with it?" Mary asked.

"Oh I just put the bits on the fire—you couldn't have repaired it. It was a bit dark and gloomy anyway—I expect mother has a mirror or something to hang in its place."

Terry felt sure that John wouldn't have let Johnny drive the horse, but he didn't like to mention it. However, Thomas McMahon came to pay his usual Sunday visit and said, "I saw Johnny driving past early the other morning—he's a lucky man to have a horse and trap like that—it's a real beauty."

John and Jane went and saw Mary and Terry that evening in their own house. John asked Terry, and he got the truth. Terry gave him his opinion, and Mary told them about the picture falling down. She didn't believe him, and she thought some of his friends were coming to the farm at night as well.

They decided that Johnny had better live at home. Johnny was angry—he was angry with his father for putting the £100 William had left him in the bank. He didn't know how to get it out, and he'd caught the urge to gamble—but he had to go home and come to work daily. John let him have his wages as usual, but he was still unhappy about the picture.

26

Little Eleanor, nearly nine years old now, announced at tea time that Thomas was going to marry her when she was eighteen.

"Indeed," said Kathleen, "you don't marry the first man who asks you."

Johnny sneered, "How many have you turned down, Kathleen— you're nearly eighteen."

"That is enough!" John shouted. "Go to your room Johnny. I will be up to see you shortly. Kathleen, dry your tears—there are dozens of men out there would love to marry you, but what would we do without you?"

Kathleen's very plain face was blotched with tears.

John looked round his family. He wished his brother William had lived—life was harder now. Jane hated the half mile walk every day to the farm, and Mary, good as she was, didn't work the same way as Jane.

John spent an hour upstairs with Johnny. He never hit any of the children, but he was sorely tempted this time. Johnny was so hard and cold—he wasn't a bit sorry for hurting Kathleen, and he was glad he had driven the horse. He was 15 years old, and to John he seemed worldly wise and slightly scruffy—not his clothes or his face and hands, John thought, but he looked shop-soiled.

Joe was still living with them, and one day John said to him, "I have to go to Castle Archdale tomorrow—would you like to come?"

"Yes, I'd love it," he replied. I've passed the big gates once or twice. I'd like to see it."

"Robert will take us to the station and we will be met at Ennis-killen—I don't think his lordship is in residence at the moment, so we'll be able to have a look round. I know the steward well."

"Where does his lordship live when he's not there?" asked Eleanor.

"He has a house in London and he sits in the House of Lords."

Eleanor couldn't make it all out. A castle in Ireland, a house in London, and he had to sit in the House of Lords—didn't they have any chairs in the London house? Everyone laughed, and her father ex-plained it to her.

Next day, John and Joe set out. It was a grand adventure for Joe—he had never seen a house like this one. John told him about the horses, and the hunting and the shoots that took place there. The King had been over to stay there before now. Joe was wide-eyed. They were met at Enniskillen by a sturdy man of about 45 years. He had a buggy and horse—John sat on the seat with him, and Joe sat behind.

Jack Wilson had worked on the estate all his life, and his father before him. He was now the steward, and he had a huge staff who respected him.

"What is the job?" John asked.

"Well," said Jack, "his lordship was up at Castle Sanderson last time he was over, and he greatly admired the gun cases you did. He was impressed by the locking system—you can't be too careful with guns. Also, he thinks there is a bit of woodworm in the library. He may have to replace all the shelves in there. The furniture was all treated and shows no sign, but the shelves are massive and I found a bit of worm on the left hand side. You might have to sleep here while you're doing it."

John hoped it wouldn't come to that, but there was a lot of work there and good pay, and he never turned down a job if he could help it. He realised he didn't really need the money, but he felt the money from William belonged to the farm. So he carried on as usual.

Jack was curious about Joe—he didn't know where he came into the picture—but when they reached home he said, "Come in—the wife will have a cup of tea ready before we start."

Mrs Wilson greeted them, and introduced her daughter, Mary Ann—a blonde girl of about fifteen.

"When you finish your tea, Joe, Mary Ann will show you round the place," Jack said. "Do you like horses?"

"Yes sir," Joe replied.

"Well, show him the stables. Peter the groom will be around."

"I hope so," said Mary Jane, "the horses scare the wits out of me."

When they went out, John told him the whole sad story of how Joe came to be living with him.

"I feel he ought to be working," John said. "Mind you, he does his fair share and more around the house and in the garden, but he should be learning a trade or earning a bit. I don't want to push him—he's been pushed enough. I thought a look around this place might help him decide what he wants—that's why I brought him today."

"Well, if he likes horses," Jack said, "I want a stable lad. We have a small stud farm here, and her ladyship is talking about breeding Shetlands. We could do with another pair of hands. There are six fellows already, but there is a lot of work. Let's wait and see his reaction to what he sees."

Mary Ann took him around till they came to a big yard with cobble-stones and a long row of horse boxes down each side. Over the half door of each box a beautiful horse looked out, and just by the gate was a small office where a wiry little man sat at a desk with a big filing cabinet nearby.

"Mr Monk, this is Joe," said Mary Ann. "Daddy asked if you would show him the horses and tell him anything he wants to know."

"How do, lad," said Peter Monk, "wait a minute and then we'll go. I must file these details before I forget them."

Mary Ann looked at Joe. "I'll come back for you in half an hour," she said.

"Aren't you coming too?" he asked.

Peter Monk laughed, "Mary Ann can't stand horses, and one day maybe she will tell me why."

She blushed and went out. When she was seven years old and playing outside, she had seen the stallion mount a little mare. It had horrified her, and she'd hated horses ever since.

Peter took Joe down the lines of boxes, explaining which ones were the brood mares and which were geldings.

"They're not like farm horses," said Joe.

"No," said Peter, and told him they were hunters mostly. At the end, around the corner, was a big box on its own, and a big bay head looked out at them. "This is Torbay the stallion, and father to some of the best horses in the country. Be careful, he gets snappy if some of his mares are in season."

They walked on to where there were empty boxes. "This is where the Shires are kept. They are out ploughing today, six of them. The ploughman sees to them, but my lads groom them and keep an eye on them."

Joe asked a lot of questions and Peter could see how interested he was. He would have stayed talking all day, but Mary Ann returned and took him around the gardens. There were miles of greenhouses and wonderful tropical plants. The humidity in there amazed Joe. The gardener explained the heating system, a coke furnace with hot water pipes running along. The pools of water with tropical fish were really there to create the humidity.

Joe was fascinated, but he couldn't forget the horses.

When they got back to the house, Jack said, "Well, what do you think?"

"To tell you the truth," said Joe, "I had no idea what a complicated business breeding horses can be. I never really thought about them before they were trained and fit for driving."

"Well Joe, we need a young lad to work in the stables. I must warn you that it is seven days a week and it is very hard work. What do you think?"

"I'd love it," Joe said, "but where would I live?"

"There are rooms over the stables—quite good rooms, but I think you are a bit young. The four boys who live up there are older than you, and they are a tough bunch. Peter has had to go over there and break up a fight once or twice. Leave it with me. I must, of course, ask Peter if he thinks you are suitable."

He turned to John. "When can you start on the gun room?"

"A week on Monday would give me time to finish what I'm doing. I'll ask my wife to keep an eye on Robert, and if he has time perhaps Robert could come and give me a hand here. I don't want to be away from home any longer than I can help. Jane and Kathleen are both a bit overworked just now."

When John and Joe got home, Joe was so full of excitement he couldn't stop talking.

"You lucky devil," Johnny said, "I'd love to work with horses."

"Don't be too optimistic," John said, "remember, he has to talk with Peter Monk."

"Yes, alright," said Joe, "but I got on well with him too."

Three days later a letter arrived from Jack Wilson. Peter Monk was happy to have Joe on his staff. The coachman and his wife would let him lodge with them until he was a bit older, and John could bring Joe along with him on Monday.

Joe was cock-a-hoop. He kissed the girls and hugged Jane, and dashed about packing his clothes.

Jane said, "You will have to tell your parents."

Joe stopped dead. "I'm not going down to the house. If mother comes on Sunday, I'll tell her. She can tell him what she likes."

"Joe, you should go and see him," Jane pleaded.

"No, I never want to see him again, ever."

Margaret and the girls came on Sunday afternoon, and Joe told them all about Castle Archdale and how he was going to work there.

"Oh Joe, no—not you! You will only be a stable boy. Come home and go back to school. My son a stable boy—how will I tell my father or my friends or James," his mother pleaded.

"Don't tell them then," Joe said, "what do I care about your friends? Everyone knew how he treated me, but no-one except the Scarletts did anything about it—not even you, mother."

Margaret cried when she left. She wanted so much for Joe to come home. Lots of fathers beat their sons—why couldn't things be easier? She told the girls not to tell James. "I'll tell him myself, at the right time."

It was late November. Margaret went out to her garden and started to dig over the vegetable patch, and she was working away when James arrived home from school. He came down the garden to finish it for her. She handed him the fork and sat down on the steps. He looked across the garden and said, "We could ask Joe to dig that bit by the hedge, and plant some spring cabbage—what do you think?"

"Joe won't be back," she said, "he's got a job at Castle Archdale working with the horses—he starts tomorrow morning."

"Our son a stable boy, mucking out and grooming? My God, is that boy really mine?"

"Yes, he really is yours and mine, James—our love child, do you remember? It was a bad start—let us hope it ends better. William tells me he is going to study Law at university—that should make you feel better. I only hope he is as happy as Joe. I've never seen Joe look better—you wouldn't recognise him, he looks the picture of health."

"It's all John Scarlett's fault," said James. "He's just a peasant at heart. In spite of his money and grand house, he's just a bloody peasant!"

• • •

Joe was called at 5.30 the morning after his first arrival, and he mucked out and wheeled barrow-loads of manure till his arms ached. He carried fresh straw for bedding, helped with the feeds, and spent a hard afternoon in the tack room. There was so much harness—it was a massive room—rosettes on the walls and riding equipment everywhere.

At six o'clock in the evening, Peter told him to go. He had driven him hard all day, but he believed in starting the way he was going to go on. Joe dragged himself to the coachman's cottage, and Mrs McGuire greeted him saying, "There's hot water, soap and a towel in the scullery—clean yourself up, and then come in to your tea."

Joe stripped off his shirt and washed down to his waist. He put the basin on the floor, rolled up his trousers and, sitting on the stool, put his feet into the basin. It was bliss. He found a clean shirt by the towel, tidied his hair, and found the McGuires waiting to start their evening meal.

They were a childless couple, both well over sixty, and Joe liked them on sight. They had talked to him the night before, and Joe had told them a bit about himself. He didn't tell everything—he still couldn't talk calmly about it.

About a week later when he came into the yard, Joe could hear the stallion Torbay whinnying, and a little mare called Zelda answering.

"Zelda is in season again," said Peter. "We didn't mate her three months ago, but I think we will have to this time. She's only four years old, and small, but his lordship agreed when we talked about it. Joe, you and Benny can watch. Harry will bring out the mare and I will bring Torbay. I want you to note how we handle the horses. It's a dangerous business for horses and man, so stand well back near the wall and take note."

Harry brought out the little mare on a halter, and Peter came out with Torbay. He was prancing and screaming, and raced up to the mare and tried to mount her, but she moved round. He tried again, and she kicked out and moved again, but Torbay suddenly grabbed her neck in his teeth. He mounted her, and rode her savagely, and then whinnied fondly, and it was over.

Joe felt a bit sick—also he had felt a stirring in his loins. He put his hands down his trouser pockets, and noticed that Benny had done the same.

Benny nudged him and grinned. "Did you get an itch, Joe?" he said. "Don't worry, we all do—even old Peter, and he's been at it for years."

Joe was told he could have a whole day off once a month. The boys all liked Sunday, so Joe thought Saturday would be best. He wanted to go and see the Scarletts, and there were no trains on Sundays.

When John had said 'goodbye' to him, he had put a £5 note into Joe's hand. Joe protested—he didn't need it. John had said, "Everyone needs money. You're on your own now. If you need anything, buy it." Joe had bought a bicycle. It cost him £1, and he could ride it now, having fallen off a few times, so he could ride to Enniskillen station, put it into the guard's van, and ride it home when he got off at the little local station at Redhills.

He turned up at 11 o'clock one Saturday. Anna was sitting on the garden seat shelling peas, and Joe sat down beside her. She admired the bicycle. Kathleen came round the corner on her way over to the farm, and Joe said casually, "Kathleen is a great worker."

"Yes," said Anna, "she'll make a good wife for some man."

"What about you?" Joe asked, "Will you make some man a good wife?"

She looked startled. "No!" she said, "I'll never marry. I just couldn't—and I couldn't have a baby, I would be terrified. No, definitely no. I'll stay as I am."

Joe looked at her. He thought she was so beautiful—her soft white skin and pink cheeks, and small red mouth and great hazel eyes—but she seemed to be untouchable. Little Eleanor gave him a hug, and Kathleen kissed his cheek, but Anna didn't make contact at all.

John and Jane were delighted to see him, and wanted to know all about the job. He didn't tell them about Torbay and Zelda—he thought about it often, but he couldn't talk about it. He thought Jane looked tired—she was working hard now, and although no-one mentioned it, he suspected that Johnny was a worry.

Joe went back after tea. His mother hadn't come, although he had written to tell her he was visiting. But he didn't really miss her.

John and Jane sat quietly for a while after he had gone. Anna and Eleanor were in bed, Kathleen was visiting a friend, and Robert, now turned 17, was seeing a girl. She was a nice girl from a decent family. She and Robert had gone to school together, and both parents approved of them meeting, but only in each other's homes.

John was at last back home, finished with the work at Castle Archdale, and he was worried about Jane.

"We can't go on racing over to the farm," he said to her. "What do you think we should do? You're tired, and are not your old self at all. I've spent a lot of time and lost a lot of sleep thinking about it."

"I love this house," replied Jane, "but the farm has been in your family for generations. I think we ought to move into the farmhouse—it's bigger than this one and needs a bit of repair, but we can soon fix that."

"And what about this house?" John asked. "Do you want to sell it?"

"No," said Jane, "leave it—I've a feeling we might want it. We can keep it tidy and aired for now—I don't want to sell it just yet."

"I'll move the workshop over to the farm," said John, "I'll be able to help on the farm in the busy time, and Mary and Terry will be glad of the quiet. It must be so noisy in there when we are working."

He was relieved that Jane decided to move—he hated to see her so overstretched. She was a farmer's daughter and knew how to run the place. Terry was good, and Johnny would have to help a bit more.

"I wonder how Mary will take it?" Jane said. "We won't need her now."

"I'll talk to her and Terry in the morning," said John.

But Mary had been expecting this, and she was ready when John spoke to her and Terry the following day. She said she would be glad of a rest—she had worked seven days a week for over seven years. She had a sister in Bangor, county Down, who she hadn't seen for years, and who had written and asked her to come for a couple of weeks. Terry said that he, too, might be leaving. He had found it hard since William's death—he'd done his best, but lay awake at night worrying about the place.

Mary was going to have a look at suitable houses in Bangor, and they thought they might buy one and keep paying guests—just one or two people at a time, or perhaps someone permanent. Mary enjoyed looking after people, and Terry thought if he had a garden he could grow flowers for sale and vegetables for the house. He would stay on for a while if they wanted him, but he needed a guiding hand on the farm and John living there would be a great help.

So John and Jane moved to the farm. Jane brought their favourite bits of furniture and stood some of the old farm stuff in a loft in the barn. It was really a lovely house, Jane decided—she hadn't realised how much space there was. There were four bedrooms upstairs, and a small bedroom, a sitting room, dining room, kitchen and scullery downstairs. Also a washroom at the back of the house outside was well furnished too. A big barn and a smaller one, the large and cool dairy, and a byre with twelve cows. There were poultry houses for chickens and turkeys, a goose run and a great flock of ducks, cart sheds and a carriage shed with a nice trap and harness cupboard. There were two farm horses and a driving horse, a shed full of dry peat and a wood shed with sawn logs piled to the roof, a big shed full of hay, four stacks of straw ready for winter bedding for the animals, and a granary with feeding stuff.

Altogether a fine farm, Jane thought. She especially liked the downstairs bedroom with the French door, and thought that if it just had a day bed, it would be a nice little den where one could be alone sometimes. The washroom behind the kitchen was a great idea too, with its boiler and fire. The water had to be poured into the boiler, but old Jack had found a spring in the yard and had sunk a pump, so water was no trouble. The big tin bath was there, so the scullery was free all the time for cooking and washing up.

Jane and Kathleen bought wallpaper and paint, and decorated the bedrooms. Kathleen had a room to herself, Anna and Eleanor shared, as did the boys.

• • •

Two years later, Jane was sitting out in the garden under the apple tree, sewing. She looked around at the flowers and shrubs they had planted, and was very happy. She could hear the saws going in the barn. John and Robert were kept busy. It was two years since they had moved—John had taken on a young boy to learn the trade, and Terry had been replaced too. Johnny and the new man got on well together. Johnny was sixteen now. He often went out in the evenings— he never said where he was going, and Jane and John had decided to let him do what he wanted within reason. Robert was eighteen, and walking out with Eileen Dixon. Jane found her a polite girl, and Robert waited on her hand and foot. She often came over for Sunday tea. Thomas McMahon still came most Sundays—if he didn't, Eleanor was unbearable. Joe came for dinner and tea once a month. So Sunday afternoons were very jolly with all the young people around.

A few weeks later, when Jane and Kathleen had prepared for Sunday and everyone had enjoyed the meal and gone into the garden, John and Jane were in the sitting room when Robert and Eileen came in.

"We would like to talk," Robert said.

"Well, why not," said John, "sit down and we can start."

"Eileen and I would like to get married."

John was surprised. "You're only eighteen," he said.

"I know," Robert looked uncomfortable, "but we think Eileen is pregnant."

John and Jane were dumfounded. "Do your parents know?" Jane asked Eileen.

"I think mother does—I hoped you would help me to tell them. My father is going to hit the roof, and I can't face him—I'm sorry, but I just can't tell him—I'm afraid he will kill Robert and me."

After a bit more talk, Jane sat down and wrote a note to Eileen's parents. She invited them over the following evening and gave Eileen the letter to take home.

Lying in bed that night John said, "Perhaps this is why we never sold the house. They could live there and Robert can still come to work. I'll have to give him a proper wage now, but I think that's what we should do, and I'll tell the Dixons tomorrow evening—it may soften the blow. It's a shock for them."

"It's a shock for all of us," Jane said sadly, "but I will enjoy a grandchild. Eleanor is getting to be a big girl now. This friendship with Thomas worries me sometimes—she never sees anyone else when he's around."

John laughed, "She's only ten years old—she has a bad case of puppy love—she'll change."

So the Dixons came and were told the news. Robert and Eileen sat with heads bowed as Jim Dixon berated them, but John told them his plan, and a wedding day was set, and everyone agreed that nothing more could be done.

It was a pretty wedding—Eileen in a pink dress with a wide hat with flowers around it and ribbons hanging down. Her cousin was bridesmaid and Johnny was best man. Robert looked very handsome in his light grey tailored suit. There were about 40 guests and the couple went to Bangor for a week and stayed with Terry and Mary who were delighted to see them. There was tea laid up in the kitchen and so much to talk about. They had a bedroom facing the sea—neither of them had ever seen the sea, and they loved it.

Mary and Terry had bought wisely—it was a terrace house, three stories, two reception rooms at the front on the ground floor and a good sized kitchen and scullery at the back—three large bedrooms on the second floor and two big rooms at the top. Mary and Terry slept in one of the attics and Mary had made a sitting room out of the other. The three big bedrooms were for guests, and Mary said that all last year's visitors had booked up again.

"How did you know what to charge?" Robert asked.

Mary blushed. "When I stayed with my sister," she said, "I booked into a guest house for two nights, then I booked into another one for the same, and then a third one. The first was good enough, but the food wasn't all that good—the second was more expensive, but the food was good—the third was awful, terribly lumpy bed, and the milk was off at breakfast. So I went for the middle one, and I think I improved on the food—and I've had no complaints. I buy butter and cream from a farmer who comes round three times a week—also cheese. The milkman calls every morning with fresh milk, and I bake my own bread and cakes. Terry helps with the cleaning and the cooking, and he grows most of the vegetables. He sells some flowers to passers-by. He thought he was going to have a lovely life, but we are both working as hard as ever."

Terry grinned, "Don't tell your father I do the washing up," he said, "he would laugh his head off!"

Robert and Eileen came back and settled into the house. Their wedding presents were all useful—pots and pans, crockery and bedding for the most part. Jane looked at Eileen's small white hands and wondered what sort of housekeeper she would be. She didn't seem as if she had ever done much, and Jane was worried for Robert, always a good feeder with his meals always waiting for him.

And as usual, Jane was right. Robert often came home with no food ready, Eileen sitting reading saying she hadn't felt well enough to work, and Robert frying bacon and eggs for them both and clearing up afterwards. But Robert adored Eileen all his life, and no-one would have dared to criticise her. The house was dusty and the bed linen not clean, but Eileen did a little each day, and only a little. She lay in bed late and read most of the afternoon. Occasionally she cooked a meal, but Robert always washed up and cleaned the kitchen.

Jane spoke to Eileen's mother about it, but she just laughed and said that they both seemed happy enough. Jane hated to see her lovely house in such a state, so she asked Kathleen to go over and help now and then. Kathleen did, and Eileen was happy to let her. Nothing roused Eileen—she lived in her books and quarrelled with no-one.

When her son was born, she had an easy birth. They decided to call him John James, after both grandfathers. Jane went over often to see him, and sometimes found him wet and fretful. Eileen complained that he had been fretful all day.

"Does he sleep at night?" Jane asked. "Well I think so," Eileen replied, "Robert gets up to him at night so I can get my sleep." Jane wanted to shake her and thought, 'What about Robert's sleep—he works hard all day and up half the night.'

Eight months later Eileen was pregnant again. She had to rouse herself at last and look after young John who was starting to crawl. Robert looked tired all the time, and his father had a talk with both of them one day. Jane was afraid to say anything—she didn't want to lose her temper and fall out, but John called in one evening and tactfully told them that if both worked a bit harder they would both be less tired. "That boy needs a bath and a clean nappy and a cuddle, and then to be put to bed," he said. "Now, that's your job Eileen, so if you do that Robert and I will make a cup of tea, and then you can put your feet up."

To his surprise Eileen did as he said and, as far as he knew, did it every evening after that. Young John, clean, dry and fed, slept better and Robert got to sleep most of the night. Kathleen called in often, did the washing and ironing, and things improved a little. Doing the washing one day, Kathleen noticed that every single pair of Robert's socks had either a heel or a toe out. Some of them had both, and placid Kathleen showed them to Eileen. Eileen cried and sobbed out that she had never darned a sock in her life, and she had neither wool nor darning needles.

Kathleen soon put that right, and showed her how to darn. She was so awkward with a needle, Kathleen wanted to hit her—but she let her carry on and saw the funny side of it when she'd finished. Young Eleanor would have had a flea in her ear if she did anything like the cobbled job Eileen had done. She hadn't even bothered to match the colours. Brown socks darned with black, black socks darned with grey—Kathleen just gave up and went home.

The second child was another boy. Eileen breast-fed him as she had done with John. He was called Edmund after someone in Eileen's books. Robert brought John over to his mother when he came to work, Eileen's mother came to stay for a week and Robert had a meal each night. Young John became a different boy—Jane potty-trained him and he got all the attention he needed. He stayed three months at the farm and Eileen was back to her old self—reading, making cups of tea and feeding the baby every time he cried.

John brought young John back to Eileen one evening. She cried and said she couldn't cope with them both, but John showed her how young John could use his potty, feed himself, and told her firmly that she must make the effort. Jane was busy—she never had a moment to spare and she was getting too old to care for babies.

So Eileen muddled along. Some days she cleaned up a bit or cooked, but very often Robert found the beds not made and the baby wet and crying at the end of his day's work. He tried not to compare her to his mother, who had five children and the house always clean and a meal on the table. He loved her as he had from the start, and she knew it.

• • •

Joe sat on the train one Saturday and tried to sort his thoughts out. It was seven years since he'd started work at Castle Archdale and a great deal had happened—especially in the past year. Mrs McGuire, where he lodged, had died, and the old man hadn't gotten over it. To add to the troubles, Lord Archdale arrived one day with a new motor car. He drove it proudly up the drive, chugging away, a young man beside him who he later introduced as his chauffeur—but he liked to drive it himself whenever he could.

Poor old McGuire, the coachman, had less and less to do. He polished the carriage and harness every day, but was seldom needed, and his mind was beginning to go. Joe did everything he could to comfort him, but he had several frights when he couldn't find him and had to call the steward to help, and today while Joe was gone he was staying with the Wilsons.

Joe was next to Peter Monk in rank now. Peter's right hand man, Old Harry, had retired and his son Young Harry was working there. Benny had left—he wasn't a good worker and Peter had had to watch him, and they were all glad when he went. There were three new lads living in the loft and Joe was in charge of them.

He smiled to himself as he remembered Zelda. He had worried about her all through her pregnancy, and patted her and sat talking to her every chance he got. But she produced a lovely foal without any trouble, and a week later, when Joe led her out past Torbay's box, the little foal had run over and Torbay had licked his neck. Zelda gave the foal a shove in the rump with her nose and ignored Torbay completely.

Peter laughed when Joe told him: "Typical woman," he said, "nose in the air one moment, rump in the air the next."

Joe, Peter and Jack Wilson had a long talk, and Joe, much to his own surprise, said that he was thinking of getting married. He meant to ask Kathleen Scarlett to marry him.

Jack said, "That's John's eldest girl—she's a bit older than you."

"She's a good girl," said Joe. "I've talked to her a lot—she isn't as good looking as Anna, but she will make a good wife if she will have me. I'm hoping his Lordship will let me have McGuire's cottage—we can live there and look after the old man. Otherwise I'm afraid they'll put him into the asylum in Monaghan, and he wouldn't last a week there."

So Jack had asked his Lordship, and he had agreed. He gave the McGuire a pension and let him polish the coaches and harness as much or as little as he liked. Jack was relieved at this, as the old man had been on his mind.

Now, Joe was on his way to propose to Kathleen.

He would be twenty-one in a couple of weeks, so he wouldn't need his parents' permission. He had never seen his father since that awful night, and although he had seen his mother, she was polite and seemed at a loss for something to talk about. He had tried to tell her of his life and his love for the horses, but she didn't ask any questions, or ask if he was happy.

When he arrived at the farm, Jane was baking, her sleeves rolled up and her elbows deep in flour. "Where is everyone?" he asked.

"Oh, Anna and Eleanor are over at Robert's," she said "John and Robert are in the workshop, and Kathleen is in the dairy—I don't know where Johnny is, he's a bit of a mystery man these days."

So Joe went round to the dairy and found Kathleen churning. He took the handle from her, and carried on turning it while she sat down on an upturned bucket—and they took it in turns until the butter was ready.

But as far as proposing was concerned, he didn't know where to begin. At last, he blurted out, "Kathleen, would you marry me?"

She looked up in surprise—"Did I hear right, Joe? Did you ask me to marry you?"

"Yes, Kathleen—I'd like you for my wife."

She smiled, and almost looked beautiful, her fine brown eyes shining. "Well then," she said, "I accept. I'd love to marry you."

"I was afraid you'd turn me down," he confessed. "I'd heard that at least two men had asked you already."

"Oh," she said, "they wanted a worker, my money and sons—they all want sons. But I'll be no-one's slave, Joe."

"I will love and take care of you, Kathleen," he said, and kissed her.

"As I will you," she replied.

When they sat down to their meal, Joe stood up and, blushing, said, "I have asked Kathleen to marry me, and she has said 'yes.'" He turned to John and then to Jane. "I'd like your blessing."

Everyone clapped, and John was lost for words. He could have sworn that Joe would ask for Anna, but he pulled himself together and gave them the blessing.

Eleanor, now fifteen, small and dainty said, "Kathy, darling, can I be a bridesmaid."

Kathleen laughed. "It won't be a big affair," she said, "I will think about it."

Jane said, "You will have a good wedding, I promise you that—no two people deserve it more, and I hope you will both be as happy as we have been."

So it was all bustle and rush as the wedding preparations went ahead.

Jane asked John to harness the horse. She was going shopping with Kathleen. John offered to drive them, but Jane said, "We will be gone all day—you would be bored stiff. Anna and Eleanor know what has to be done in the house."

And after five or six hours, they arrived back home, the trap piled high with parcels. Jane had bought quantities of linen, table clothes, bed linen, towels, plenty of underwear and night dresses. They had bought Kathleen's wedding gown at the best shop in Clones—cream lace, very plain and very beautiful, lined with palest pink silk, and the bodice encrusted with seed pearls. There were lovely silk stockings and satin shoes, and they had bought all the material for the bridesmaid's dresses, for Anna and Eleanor were both going to be bridesmaids.

Joe wrote to tell his mother, and enclosed a letter to be sent on to William at college in Dublin inviting him to be best man. William was overjoyed to hear from his brother, and he said he would be honoured even if he had to walk the whole way.

Kathleen and her parents went down to Castle Archdale and had a look at the cottage, and met old McGuire. It was one of his better days, and he gave them a warm welcome. Kathleen noted the neglected look of the place. For over a year there had been only Joe and the old man—it needed a woman's hand.

Sitting sewing one evening, Jane said to Kathleen, "I think Joe loves you very much—do you love him?"

Kathleen looked up. "I've loved Joe since the night he came to our door. I think I just wanted to mother him then—but he's grown up so nicely. I still want to mother him, but he is as strong as I am. I made up my mind that I wouldn't run after him, and I thought he loved Anna. I couldn't have blamed him—she's so lovely—but I decided that I wouldn't marry anyone else as long as Joe stayed single. I was really surprised when he asked me, but I will make him happy, and he has promised to love and take care of me."

"He's a good man," Jane said, "you will do well together."

The wedding day dawned, slightly cloudy. John looked up at the sky at six o'clock in the morning and prayed for sunshine. He knew Kathleen could have married into one of the farming community, but Jane had told him what Kathleen had said, and though he knew Joe would never be rich, Kathleen would always be busy wherever she was—busy and happy, he thought.

At ten o'clock the sun came out and shone all day. The wedding was at eleven. Joe's mother didn't come because his father James wouldn't, although Jane and John had invited the whole family. Joe's sisters came with William, and he handed them over to Jane as he took his place next to Joe at the altar.

Kathleen came into church on John's arm. She looked radiant in her lovely dress, a matching hat, and a bouquet of cream and pink rose buds. He cheeks, usually rather pale, had a rosy glow and her eyes were like stars. Joe turned to look at her, and thought, "My God, she is lovely—why have I never noticed it before."

Jane had called in at least six women to help, and trestle tables borrowed from the church hall were spread with snowy clothes and laid out on the lawn, laden with food. And set in the middle of the dining room table was a beautiful wedding cake.

The wedding feast went on until dusk, with the bridesmaids, in cream taffeta dresses trimmed with pink ribbons and roses in their hair, enjoying the admiring glances of the young men. At the end, Jane's brother and his family drove back to Cootehill, and her sister and niece stayed on for a few days.

John had tried to treat Kathleen and Joe to a honeymoon, but they declined. Joe didn't want to desert old Mr McGuire, and Kathleen wanted to get started cleaning the cottage. "We will have a week later on," they said, so they caught a late train and were met at Enniskillen by one of the stable boys, who teased Joe all the way back.

The family sat tired and weary in the sitting room. Anna and Eleanor, still in their taffeta dresses, made cups of tea for everyone.

Jane's sister, Alice, said: "It won't be long before there's another wedding—Anna will soon be snapped up—the young men were buzzing round her like flies."

"She turns them all down," John said. "I think we have an old maid on our hands."

"She certainly doesn't encourage them," said Jane. "Sometimes I feel sorry for the poor lads—she doesn't even bother to talk to them. I saw that young Thomas holding Eleanor's hand during the afternoon.

I thought she would have got over him by now. How he will ever manage to get married I don't know—his family take his wages and can't manage without him. If Eleanor wants to marry him, she will have to take on the whole family, and that sister of his is very stuffy. I couldn't get a civil word out of her today. She said it was a terrible waste of money having a wedding like this, and that Kathleen's wedding dress would be useless afterwards."

John snorted, "I hope you told her to mind her own business."

"No, I didn't," Jane said. "I told her Kathleen and Joe were worth every penny, and that we were lucky not having to count pennies."

"What did she say to that?" John asked.

"She just sniffed and walked away."

Alice laughed. "I saw her filling her plate several times—she could have been fasting for a week."

They all giggled and talked for a while, and then everybody fell into their beds.

Joe and Kathleen sat in the cottage and drank tea, and talked about the day. Old McGuire was staying for the night with the Wilsons. Finally Joe lit the lamp, and they went up to their room. He pulled off his clothes and got into bed. Kathleen hung up her suit, picked up Joe's suit and hung that up too. Then she put her nightgown on and slipped into bed. Joe blew out the lamp. Both were totally inexperienced. He took Kathleen in his arms and kissed her gently, then more urgently, then finally made love—and it was over almost as soon as it started.

He felt like a fool. "I'm sorry about that, my love."

"Was it your first time too?" asked Kathleen.

"Yes."

"Well, we will never be able to say that again—let's get some sleep."

Kathleen cuddled up to him and was soon asleep, but Joe lay awake for a while—hoping he would improve—then he too slept.

Next morning he woke very early as usual, and looked at his sleeping wife. She had pushed the covers back, and her firm breasts were showing through the thin nightgown. Joe bent down, and kissed her throat. She opened her eyes and smiled at him, and then they made love slowly—and both were satisfied. So began their married life.

• • •

43

John and Jane were talking in bed. Jane said, "I was glad to see Eileen and the children looking so smart. That pale blue suit she was wearing was expensive, and the boys' clothes and shoes were new too."

"And Robert's shirt, and the tie—and he hadn't any darns in his socks," John laughed. "I gave him £20 to make sure they were all smart. I think she is coping better—the house was fairly clean last time I went over."

"She is going to miss Kathleen—she did most of the washing and ironing, but John will be at school soon, and Edmund is dry night and day, so there won't be so much washing," Jane remarked.

• • •

Kathleen liked old McGuire. They talked a lot, or rather he talked and she listened. It was all about the old days, working with the horses and carriage outside grand houses, the great Christmas Balls that used to be in the big house, and the staff Christmas parties. Kathleen enjoyed it all. Sometimes he forgot what he had been saying, and sometimes he fell asleep almost in the middle of sentence. Then Kathleen would tuck a rug round his knees and quietly carry on with her housework.

She was sometimes at a loss how to fill her day. Her mother had given her a brand new sewing machine, and she went into Enniskillen and bought some material and a pattern. She was making herself a skirt, and also decided to knit a matching jumper.

Jack Wilson's wife came over sometimes to see the old man. She saw the sewing machine and material on the table, and was very impressed by Kathleen's work.

"Where did you learn to make dresses?" she asked.

"My mother taught me. She's also teaching my two sisters—they can make a lot of their clothes now."

"Well," Mrs Wilson said, "I may have to ask your help soon. Mary Ann has got engaged to a young lawyer in town. They hope to get married next year. I never can find anything in the shops. I'm narrow in the shoulders and wide in the hip. Perhaps we could find a pattern—would you help me?"

"If I can," said Kathleen. "I'm not an expert, but I like things to have a nice finish, and mother was a good teacher."

• • •

Jane was busy. Anna and Eleanor had to help a lot more now, and to her surprise Eleanor buckled down cheerfully and worked from morning to night. She was small and wiry, and tireless. She churned, made the butter, fed the chickens, gathered eggs and packed them, fed the calves and milked the cows. Anna cooked and cleaned the house. Jane was proud of them both.

Johnny was the only one who worried the parents. He was twenty-one now, and had asked John for his £100. John asked him what he wanted it for. He said he hoped to buy a couple of horses, train them, feed them up a bit and sell them at a profit. He was friendly with a horse dealer who had told him a few things to look for.

"Have we enough grazing for any more horses?" asked John.

Johnny had his answer. He could rent a couple of fields from a local farmer—they were there for the taking.

John knew the horse dealer, and although he didn't know anything bad about him, he thought he was a bit of a 'chancer'—loud of voice and loud in dress, bold check jackets and bright ties. He didn't like him, but he gave Johnny the money.

Johnny had nothing but contempt for Robert. He said he was hen-pecked. He hadn't wanted to go to Kathleen's wedding—he thought Joe was a fool tying himself down with a wife. He hardly noticed Robert's two sons, and he had stopped going to church.

He didn't show John the two horses he had bought, and Jane had to have a word with him about the farm work. He never went into the workshop, nor showed any interest in what his father and Robert were doing, but John and Jane walked over to where Johnny was training his horses, and John had to admit that Johnny knew a good horse. He talked to him, and was surprised how much he knew, and how well he could ride. The hard-hearted Johnny was gone, and his gentle care of the animals impressed both John and Jane.

• • •

Kathleen made Mrs Wilson's dress for Mary Ann's wedding. They had shopped together and chosen a lovely pale lilac velvet. Mrs Wilson was fair-haired, like her daughter, with lazy blue eyes. The pattern was two-piece, a straight skirt, very plain, and jacket top with a peplum, almost a bustle, at the back and leg-of-mutton sleeves.

Kathleen got up at 5.30 am, when Joe did. She had her house in order and the bread baked by 10 o'clock. After a cup of tea for herself and old McGuire, she worked until 1 o'clock. A quick snack, then back to work until 4.30 pm. She never worked at her machine in the evening—firstly because her evenings were for Joe, to listen and talk about their day, and secondly because paraffin lamps gave a poor light, and she wanted the dress to be perfect.

She made the bridesmaid's dress as well—a pretty sprigged cotton, flounced from waist to floor. The Wilsons were delighted.

Lord and Lady Archdale gave the wedding breakfast at the castle, and opened the French windows for people to walk through into the gardens. They both attended the church service. His Lordship said to his wife, "Be careful what you wear—you mustn't outshine Mrs Wilson." But even her Ladyship was impressed by the bride's mother's rigout. She complimented her. When she heard who made it, she came over to Kathleen, who was wearing the brown velvet dress she had made up for coming home from her own wedding. It was very smart, with Irish lace collar and cuffs. She praised her work.

A few days later, Kathleen was invited to the castle and found a lot of orders waiting for her. Dresses for the two children, nightgowns for Mylady, and the Governess wanted a dress. Kathleen was quite prepared to do it for nothing, but her Ladyship was firm, and Kathleen was very surprised at what she was earning—and she was busy all the time.

One year later, Kathleen sat hand-sewing while Mr McGuire was talking. She answered him now and then—he was talking a lot today. She looked up at him and smiled, and he smiled back—then suddenly he said, "Well, goodnight Mrs McGuire."

She laughed, and answered, "Goodnight Mr McGuire." Joe had told her that he and his wife never used their Christian names—always Mr and Mrs.

He closed his eyes and she tucked the rug round him. An hour later, she came over and found he had died in his sleep.

Two days later he was buried in Belleek churchyard. Every man on the estate attended—he had been there all his life. His only relative, a brother, came, and after the funeral took his few possessions. Joe told him to take whatever he wanted, but apart from a few photographs, cuff-links and a tie-pin, he left whatever else there was. His Lordship handed Kathleen an envelope after the funeral. Inside was a 'thank you' letter and £50. She had solved the problem of what to do with a sick old man with nowhere to go.

Kathleen had come to love him, and missed him. She wished she had a child, she told Joe. She was nearly 25 years old—she hoped she hadn't left it too late.

Joe said, "Don't give up hope—it will happen, I feel sure. I would love a child—it would complete our happiness, and you will make a wonderful mother."

• • •

Eleanor was singing in the dairy. She had a good voice—both she and Anna were in the choir—and stood happily turning the handle of the churn.

Her mother came in and took a turn. "You sound cheerful, child," she said.

"I'm eighteen in two weeks time, and Thomas is going to go down on one knee and ask me to marry him—he has promised to do it properly."

"Where are you two going to live when you get married," Jane asked.

Eleanor's face clouded. "He would like me to move in with his family," she said, "but I don't know. Jeannie is a bit unfriendly and his father is snappy, but his mother is really nice."

Jane said, "Your father will never agree to your going there. We both know you work hard and willingly, but there is plenty of everything here—we are very comfortable and well fed. It will be different there—they hardly have enough to eat."

"I know," Eleanor agreed, "I've been to Sunday tea a few times and it was very plain fare—not like your Sunday tea table, groaning with the weight of all the lovely things you bake."

"Well, food costs money," Jane said, "and if you haven't much money, you cut down on the food—that's life!"

Thomas asked Eleanor to marry him two days after her eighteenth birthday.

John talked seriously to them both. He couldn't agree to let Eleanor live with the McMahons. He found old Tom difficult—never a smile for anyone. Jeannie was 32, and a sour old maid. Mrs McMahon was a nice woman—she deserved better than her husband and Jeannie.

Thomas loved his mother, but John stood firm.

John was making a walnut cabinet for a Major Kells. The Major came into the workshop and, having approved the work, asked John how his family were. John went through them all until he came to Eleanor, and he told the Major his dilemma.

"Has the boy any training, apart from helping his father?" he asked.

"Oh yes," said John, "he has been working in the Castle gardens for ten years—he is third gardener there, I believe. They have twelve gardeners in all."

"Well now," the Major said, "an army friend of mine, Major Musson, has a small estate just outside Lisburn and he wants a gardener. He hasn't many cottages, but there is a fine gate lodge vacant. Shall I get in touch with him?"

So John, after hearing from Major Kells that Major Musson would be delighted to have Thomas and Eleanor, put the proposition to Thomas.

Thomas saw the answer to his problem—he also saw himself having to tell his parents he was about to leave home. He earned 7/6d per week and was now about to earn 15/-, but how could he tell them? They needed his money, but he had loved Eleanor for so long, and they had waited patiently for her eighteenth birthday.

Eleanor was lively—he had seen other fellows watch her at the parish dances, and he had hardly been able to get near to ask her for a dance. Anna was cold and beautiful, but Eleanor joked and laughed with everyone. Anna had her suitors too, but she didn't want them. She was the same age as Thomas, twenty-two, and she still said she didn't want to marry.

John and Jane talked it over and made their decision. They invited Tom McMahon and his wife to come to Sunday dinner. They didn't invite Jeannie, but Thomas was asked. After dinner, John took Tom into the sitting room. He told him about Major Musson's offer. He explained that, in his opinion, the McMahons couldn't feed yet another mouth. He offered Tom twenty-five pounds and suggested what he might do with it—another cow perhaps, or more poultry—whatever he thought would help his income.

Old Tom hated to be beholden to John, but £25 was a fortune. He had hoped to get Eleanor's dowry of £100, but he knew when he was beaten. He accepted the offer, and Thomas was free.

Eleanor was very sensible about her wedding. She wanted a dress she could get some wear out of afterwards, so she bought a Donegal tweed suit and a white frilly blouse. She carried a white prayer book and had a spray of red rose buds on her lapel. Jane had wanted to dress her up, but Eleanor said what she wore didn't matter.

She has loved Thomas since she was six years old, thought Jane, and she would get married in a potato sack if I would let her.

John had made some furniture for them, and Jane gave her a sewing machine, just as she had done for Kathleen. She hoped it would be as useful as Kathleen's had proved to be.

There was a great reception, with food aplenty. Thomas's sisters, Minnie and Barbara, came home from Belfast. They were nice girls, very different to Jeannie who sniffed at everything. There were friends and relations from all over the country, and that evening Thomas and Eleanor caught the tram to Lisburn to begin their new life.

Major Musson met them. They had met before, when they went to see the cottage. It was partly furnished, and John had made them some more furniture and put it on the tram. It was now all in place. The Mussons had left a box of groceries in the kitchen for them, and milk and bread: "Just to start you off," the major smiled.

Eleanor said, "I'm going to be very happy here—what about you, Thomas?"

"I'm happy when you are, my love," he replied.

Two weeks later, Mrs Musson looked in on Eleanor. She was sitting embroidering a blouse she had made. Mrs Musson was impressed: "You're very good," she said.

"Mother taught the three of us to make dresses. I can embroider and I can make Irish lace as well. Mother taught us everything to do with housekeeping—she learned from her mother."

So, like Kathleen, Eleanor got orders from the big house. They didn't have a large staff, just a cook, parlour maid and housemaid living in, and a girl daily from the village to help. The Major had a car, and there was a horse and buggy which one of the farm hands took into Lisburn weekly for the shopping. He called in on Eleanor each week and got her shopping as well, and once or twice she had gone with him, glad of the lift. It was a two mile walk, and uphill coming back—so everything went well.

They went to the local church on Sunday mornings, Eleanor in her nice tweed costume, Thomas in his navy blue suit. They were a handsome pair. Soon everyone knew who they were, and Eleanor joined the choir. They were married just over a year when Eleanor got out of bed one morning and felt sick. She was normally a very healthy girl, and was surprised when she had to run out of doors suddenly. She didn't feel very well until lunchtime. The cook called in during the afternoon, and Eleanor said she must have eaten something that had disagreed with her. The cook laughed and said, "I think you are going to have a baby"—and she was right.

The sickness went after a couple of weeks, and Eleanor in her weekly letter to her mother told her the good news. Jane and John were delighted, and wrote back with instructions on what to do and what not to do. Jane wrote, "Don't stretch up hanging curtains, and don't lift anything heavy. You must take care of yourself. Kathleen and Joe are coming on Saturday—I'm sure they will be pleased."

Eleanor laughed as she read. She wished Kathleen had a baby too—she hoped she wouldn't be envious. But Kathleen was able to tell her parents that at last she too was pregnant. Eleanor's was due in March, and Kathleen's in April. John said, "It never rains but it pours—I hope they don't both have twins!"

Kathleen didn't have an easy pregnancy—she was sick right the way through. Eleanor, on the other hand, put it out of her head until she could ignore it no longer. Both of them knitted and stitched and made all their baby clothes. So too did Jane and Anna.

Jane was pleased for them. She missed the Sunday gatherings—she often cooked and prepared food and nobody came. She wished Eleanor and Thomas were nearer—she hadn't seen them since they got married, but Eleanor seemed happy.

Anna, without her sisters, talked more now. She didn't get any more callers—she had made it clear to everyone that she didn't want marriage.

Johnny was still buying and selling horses. He bought rather flashy clothes, and had gone over to O'Reilly's again. He still liked to gamble, but the lads he used to play cards with hadn't changed—they were like boastful children, and he had grown away from them.

He started gambling with new friends. Sometimes he won as much as £50 during an evening, but he quite often lost every penny—then he would sell a horse or two and leave the cards for a week, but he always went back. He had been involved with women from time to time, but in his heart he despised them. They fell for his good looks and easy manner, then he tired of them and would pass them in the street without even seeing them. He never brought any girl home to meet his family. John took on another workman for the farm, and Johnny came and went as he pleased.

In March, Jane went to stay with Eleanor and saw her through the birth. She had a 7 lb boy, who they named John Thomas after both granddads, and she was up and about at the end of a week. The nurse and Jane tried to keep her in bed, but she wouldn't listen. She was back to normal, and a month later her waist was back to 22 inches. She told Thomas that if she had laid in bed for another week, she would have been as fat as a pig.

Jane went home and told John all about it. He said, "She's not very big, but she's tough." Thomas was as proud as a peacock. The baby was placid and fed and slept, and life was good.

In April, Jane went to stay with Kathleen. She had lost her bloom and looked drawn. She asked all about Eleanor and the baby. Seven pounds seemed a good size. She was glad Eleanor had had an easy birth, but poor Kathleen had a terrible time. The pains were bad and went on and on from Monday afternoon until Tuesday midday. Her son arrived at 12.45 on Tuesday 11th April. He was 9 lbs, he was red, and he screamed his head off. Kathleen wanted to breast-feed him, but had to put him on a bottle. He cried all night and slept a while in the mornings, then cried most of the afternoon and evening. Jane had never come across such a child—she'd had five children, all very different, but Samuel Joseph was something new.

Jane went home, and Kathleen wondered how she was ever going to cope with Sam. She asked Joe if he would sleep in the spare room now her mother had gone. She said he would need his rest, as he had to go to work. What she really meant was that she never wanted to be pregnant again. She couldn't forget the pain. Joe, always reasonable, said he would take his turn getting up in the night for Sam, but Kathleen, weary as she was, wanted to see Sam for herself. She let Joe hold him for a little while when she dished up the evening meal. She wrapped him up in blankets and shawls and woolly jackets, and Joe only ever saw his face.

When Sam was four months old, her ladyship sent down. She wanted to see Kathleen. It was Saturday and Joe was at home. Kathleen was prepared to carry Sam up to the castle, but Joe said, "Leave him with me—I'll look after him." Kathleen looked anxious. Joe laughed, "I'm quite capable, Kathleen—I won't drop him or poison him—anyway he's asleep, so you go on. I promise you he'll be alright."

Half an hour later, Sam woke up and started crying. Joe picked him up. He looked hot, so Joe took off the woolly bonnet. His hair was dark with sweat. Joe then unwrapped him and took off the woolly leggings. He laid a blanket on the floor and lay the baby down. At first Sam whimpered—he didn't know how to cope with so much freedom—then he waved his arms and kicked his feet and cooed. Joe sat watching him. He's a lovely boy, he thought—Kathleen will soon have to let him move about a bit.

Kathleen came back and was horrified. "How dare you?" she cried, "he'll catch a cold."

"Use your sense, woman," Joe shouted back, "it's midsummer— when are you going to treat him like a boy—he's not a doll. And when am I going to get back into my own bed? I'm sick of all this—we used to be so happy, but now I'm like a lodger."

Kathleen cried, and they made up. She didn't want to sleep with him, but there was no excuse not to.

She was as frigid as she could be, letting Joe kiss just her cheek, pushing his arms away when he tried to cuddle her. In the end he used to turn his back and go to sleep, and that became the pattern of their lives.

Sam would wake up screaming—Kathleen would take him into her bed, and if he slept, she kept nudging Joe in case the baby got smothered. At last, Joe simply went into the spare room and mother and baby slept in the double bed. Kathleen still loved Joe and longed for a hug, but she was terrified of having another child. Sam was a handful, and she couldn't take the risk.

Joe buried himself in his work and tried not to think of where his marriage was going.

• • •

Jane decided to get the family together for Christmas. She wrote to Kathleen and Eleanor to see if they could get a few days. Joe had no trouble, Peter said he deserved a break, and Thomas had very little to do in the garden in winter, so Jane and Anna were making great preparations for a Christmas to remember.

They all arrived on Christmas eve. John had been longing to see his grandchildren. Eleanor's little John was still brown, because Eleanor stripped him and he lay out in his cradle under the apple trees all summer—he was sturdy and brown and wasn't shy at all. Sam was much bigger, and was a fretful, pale child.

On Christmas Day, Eleanor mashed up potatoes and minced goose and gravy and vegetables for John. Kathleen was horrified—she still bottle-fed Sam. Jane agreed with Eleanor—if he ate it and had no ill effects and slept all night, that proved it. But Kathleen still stuck to milk, and Sam cried most of the time.

On Boxing Day, John senior asked Joe, Thomas and Robert to go out with the guns. There were only two guns, but they enjoyed themselves and brought back several rabbits and a brace of pheasants. The three young men were sitting in the kitchen and Joe said, "I'm thinking of joining the army." Robert said he had been thinking the same thing. Thomas admitted that he hadn't thought about it, but there was a war on. Thomas's two best friends had joined already. The three men talked on about it. Robert was alright—he knew his parents were there for Eileen. Joe wasn't sure if Kathleen would be allowed to live on in the cottage if he was gone. Thomas was sure that Eleanor could live on in the gate lodge, but he knew she would be devastated if he went.

They all returned home for New Year. In the middle of January, Jane wrote and told Eleanor that Robert and Joe were gone to war. Kathleen was allowed to live in the cottage until he came back. Eileen was still weepy, but John had a talk with her and she was getting used to looking after the house and the children on her own.

Thomas longed to go to war too. He wondered if Robert and Joe thought he was a coward. He spoke to Major Musson about it—the major two sons were already in the army and were in France.

He thought it would be over soon. "Wait six months," he said to Thomas, "and if you still want to go then I will let Eleanor stay in the cottage."

Thomas decided to wait. He did his work and nursed his little son who was walking now—a bit unsteady, but definitely on his feet. He took his gun one morning very early, hoping to bag a few rabbits, but coming back he was walking along a ditch and slipped down a rabbit burrow. He tried to get up, but his leg wouldn't hold him. He crawled and dragged his leg and shouted for help. A workman heard him and helped him home. The doctor came and told him he had a broken ankle.

Eleanor had her hands full. Thomas looked after young John as well as he could, but Eleanor was pregnant again and wasn't as well this time. It took Thomas nearly six months to get back on his feet and walk. He went to the Recruiting Office, but was turned down as he was still limping slightly.

In 1916, Eleanor had another son. This one was different from John—he didn't sleep as well, he didn't cry very often, but he was awake and bright-eyed and was really a very beautiful child. They christened him Harold.

One day Thomas came in at midday for his lunch and Eleanor handed him a letter which had been delivered that morning. It was from Jeannie—their mother had fallen and broken her hip—she was confined to bed, and there was nobody to milk the cows. She had never tried, and old Tom had no intention of starting. A neighbour was helping out, but Thomas and his family would have to come home. Jeannie didn't know what would become of them if Thomas didn't come home.

So Thomas and Eleanor and their two babies came back to Rahulton. Poor old Jane was in bed in the bedroom next to the kitchen, Thomas and Eleanor had their bed in the parlour, and the children were in a small bed in the room with them.

Jeannie prepared the dinner next day—a big dish of boiled potatoes and spring onions. Eleanor was dismayed for them all—she was used to more than this. She asked if little John could have a bit of butter with his potatoes and the old man glared at her, but she got it.

Later she said to Thomas, "Our children will starve here—take your gun and get us a few rabbits or something." So he went out early, and came back with two rabbits and two pheasants. His father went mad: "Those pheasants belong to the estate—we will be in trouble if the Colonel finds out." Thomas said he shot them on his own fields, but the old man kept on about it for days.

Jeannie belonged to a little gathering of maiden ladies called 'The Girls' Friendly Society', or GFS for short. They met every Wednesday afternoon in the old school house, so from two o'clock until five Eleanor had the house to herself. She was nearer to her own mother now, and when she went over to see her she always came back with some food, which she hid in her bedroom.

One Wednesday, she took a tray into the old lady with nice thin soda bread and butter and a slice of fruit cake. Old Jane smiled and said, "This is not the gaffer's cooking," and Eleanor told her that her mother had given it to her. They became great friends, and Jane told her how pleased she was to have her and Thomas and how she loved the children. So Wednesday became party day, and they joked about Jeannie's cooking.

Sadly, the old lady died about a year later. Eleanor missed her, but she was gradually taking over the cooking and intended to do all the housekeeping. Jeannie stayed in bed after her mother's death, but Eleanor was pregnant once again and she spoke quite sharply to both her in-laws. They decided to go and stay for a while with Minnie in Belfast, so Thomas and Eleanor were happier. They had to work hard and food and money were often scarce, but they managed.

Their daughter was born in 1919. They named her Florence, but she was always called Polly. All the family were pleased—a grand-daughter for Jane and John at last, and such a pretty one.

Jeannie and old Tom came back, but Eleanor told them she was going to do the cooking and look after the money. The old man asked her to get a bottle of whiskey for him each week—she said, "No." He said, "I need it to help me sleep," and she said there was no money for drink: "Go out and give Thomas a hand—the work and fresh air will make you sleep."

She and Jeannie continued to quarrel—Thomas was at his wit's end, but Eleanor stuck to her guns and bought extra poultry and had a little sow and some turkeys. She was determined to live a bit better and make sure her children had enough to eat.

In September 1920, Eleanor had another son, and old Tom, who hardly ever noticed the children, took a shine to this one. They named him Robert, but he was called Bob. He was a good child. The old man carried him around and even took his pram out to the fields with him.

• • •

When the Fenian uprising occurred in Dublin in 1916, it seemed a long way away, but in fact there was a feeling of unrest everywhere.

It was a well known fact that no Catholics on the Sanderson Estate had ever been evicted—indeed the Sanderson family had provided food and shelter for homeless people—but that didn't make any difference to the young hot-heads who hated the English, and in particular the landed gentry.

One day in 1917, four big stacks of straw had been burned down in the estate yard—it could have been an accident, but nobody believed that. The Colonel asked his invalid wife if she would go and live in England—they had property near Newbury in Berkshire—but she said no, she was well-liked by everyone so she felt no-one would harm her.

However, three months later, two horses were found in the pad-dock with their throats cut—two beautiful hunters—and Mrs Sander-son agreed to leave. If someone was vile enough to slay innocent horses, they were capable of killing her. She left with her nurse, and the colonel's solicitor arrived at the castle. They were there nearly a month. One day the colonel called in his tenants and handed them all the deeds to their houses and land. He also gave them about 15 acres of extra grazing land. Old Thomas McMahon was now the proud owner of a house and 40 acres. After that all the furniture and fittings at the castle were shipped to England. A year later the British Army—known as the Black and Tans—moved into the castle to keep law and order.

Thomas McMahon joined the 'B Specials' and Eleanor, pregnant again in 1920, had to sit with her back to the wall between the window and the front door while the Fenians peppered the door and windows with bullets.

• • •

Robert Scarlett got back from the war in December 1918—just getting home in time for Christmas. He found Eileen had become quite a good housekeeper and his boys almost young men. He felt proud as he looked at them—they were shy at first, but were soon talking. His parents were 80, and pleased to have him back safe and well.

John told him to take his time in coming back to work. It had been slow during the four years of war—people just wanted peace, not new furniture. But money wasn't a problem to John—he had been drawing money out from time to time. Johnny still lived at home, but seldom bothered about the farm. He had made quite a lot of money during the war years when horses were in demand.

Robert asked Jane if she could have the boys overnight. He and Eileen were going to Portadown and would be back the next day. He didn't say why he was going, and Jane wisely didn't ask him. Eileen was a bit mystified too—he just told her to wait and see.

He took her to a busy street and stopped at a shop which was empty. It was a good brick building with rooms on the second floor. He got the keys from a solicitor and went through the place. There was a large empty room behind the shop, and outside concrete steps led to the flat above. Two large bedrooms, a small bathroom and toilet, a sitting room and small kitchen.

"I'm thinking of starting my own business," he said. "I'll use the back room to make the furniture and the shop to show it. We could live very well upstairs, and it's near the school and shops." Eileen was delighted—she loved shops and hated living out in the country. The price was £550—Eileen's heart sank—where could they find that sort of money. Robert said he would try the bank for a loan. They found a cheap hotel and had a meal. In the morning they had another look—it still looked good.

"You will miss having a big house," Robert said. Eileen smiled and didn't answer. I will miss having to keep a large house clean, she thought.

They came home and told Jane and John. Jane was surprised, but John always felt that Robert would go on his own sooner or later. Robert told him he was hoping to get a loan. "No need for that," his father said, "I will give you the money. You have worked hard and learned well."

He gave him a cheque for £1,000, and Robert was over the moon—he would be able to make the shop attractive, and Eileen had a good eye for colour. She helped to paper the walls and picked a lovely red carpet. "Your furniture will look good on a nice red carpet," she insisted, and Robert, three months later, had to admit she was right. Soon the orders were coming in, most of the furniture in the shop had a SOLD sticker on it, and people often stood outside just looking.

A great many people got rich during the war—black marketeers and many others. Every street in every town had a one-legged soldier, or even one with no legs, sitting in a little cart begging or selling matches, but a lot of riff-raff were in the money, building big houses, and many came to Robert Scarlett's shop for their furniture. Eileen took the orders and kept the books. Robert took on an upholsterer and a couple of ex-servicemen to learn the business. He was working twelve hours, six days a week, but he was happy. Eileen loved to get time off and buy clothes—the boys liked their school and would soon be joining Robert in the workshops.

• • •

Joe, alas, came back to Castle Archdale. Old Peter was delighted to see him—Kathleen, too, was glad he was safely back, but Sam had slept with her while Joe was away and screamed blue murder when he was moved into the spare room. He came into his parents' bedroom two or three times during the night, and yelled when Joe firmly took him back to his own bed. Sam hated Joe—he had come back and upset everyone. Joe tried every way to get to know him, but Sam wanted to sleep with his mother and Joe was determined that he wouldn't.

One morning when they were going out and were sitting having breakfast, Joe said, "Sam, drink your milk—we have to go soon." Sam glared at him, and deliberately turned the mug of milk upside down all over the table cloth. Joe picked him up, put him over his knee, and slapped him hard. Kathleen was furious—Sam had never had a smack. Joe said, "It's time he had," and Kathleen said, "You're turning out like your father, old James Lyons—do you remember how he used to beat you?"

Joe shouted, "I'm not going to watch him waste food. A year ago I'd have crawled on a bed of nails for a mug of milk, in the trenches in France. We never saw milk or any of the things you and Sam take for granted." But that night, Joe slept in the spare room, and Sam slept in his mother's bed each night till he was twelve years old.

Eleanor invited Kathleen and Sam to come and stay. The old man and Jeannie were away, and they hadn't seen much of each other over the years. Kathleen admired little Polly—a beautiful blonde child. John and Harold were looking forward to seeing their cousin Sam, but they found him hard to play with. He wanted to be top dog, and kicked and bit them if he couldn't. At last they gave him a ducking in the stream. Kathleen was incensed how anyone could do that to her beloved son. She thought John and Harold very rough boys, and Sam stayed in and played with Polly. But Eleanor caught him pulling Polly along by her curls and she was crying bitterly, so Kathleen got a good talking to and went home a few days early.

She went to Jane and John and told them how badly Sam had been treated, and they tried to tell her she was spoiling him. "Let him stick up for himself," John said, "he'll suffer at school when you're not there." But Kathleen wouldn't listen.

John loved Eleanor's children—they were so independent, helped around the house and played for hours with a ball or a pair of old pram wheels, and spending a weekend with Grandad and Grandma Scarlett was wonderful, lots of cuddles and lovely food, and they could chatter as much as they liked. Aunt Anna was nice too—she hadn't got married, but she played with them, and she was very pretty.

In 1923, Eleanor had a daughter, her fifth child. They couldn't make up their minds what to call her. Elizabeth, they thought. They took all the children to their grandparents, and Eleanor put her sleeping baby into old John's arms. He chuckled as he looked at her—this tiny bundle, pink with a thatch of black hair. She opened her eyes—they seemed too big for her face, and she seemed to know that she had a friend here. "Call her Jessica," John said, "this is a smart little one."

"Jessica Elizabeth then," Eleanor said. John loved Jessica—she was just like Eleanor was as a baby. Eleanor had to admit to herself that this one wasn't as pretty as Polly, but she was a good baby— screamed if she was wet or hungry, but slept well, and Harold, who was seven years old, pushed her pram around the lanes. He thought she was wonderful.

• • •

When Jessica was four years old, John Scarlett had a slight stroke. He recovered, but had to be careful. He had two men in the workshop, and only did the fiddly bits himself. He walked with his grandchildren round the fields, and advised Jane who, with the help of two workmen, ran the farm.

Anna had begun to think of the future. She knew the farm would go to Johnny when her parents died, and she knew the company Johnny kept. He was likely to bring any sort of woman home, and Anna knew she would be pushed out—and she didn't know what to do. She was 35 years old, still very good-looking, and she had saved some money as well as the £100 she would get if she married. Then out of the blue, a young widower about her own age came courting. Anna liked him— he had two young sons who needed a mother. He proposed, and Anna accepted him. They had a quiet wedding and went back to his small farm near Enniskillen.

Anna had never worked so hard in her life. She began to realise what Eleanor was going through. She was up early, baking and milking, and when the boys went to school she joined her husband in the fields—they even worked by moonlight. She was kind to the boys, but they were wary—they'd had several women looking after them since their mother had died, and they wondered if this one would stay.

But Anna stayed. She never had a child, for which she was grateful, and she and George were so weary at night that they slept as soon as their heads touched the pillow.

Old John Scarlett had another stroke and died in 1929. His funeral was the biggest ever seen in the parish. Old Tom McMahon also died that year—Jeannie left for Belfast afterwards and stayed three months.

Eleanor had another son, William. He was a big child and very demanding, and in 1931 she had a last child, a little boy, and she wasn't well for a long time afterwards. The doctor told Thomas, "No more babies—Eleanor is worn out—it will take a long time to get her back on her feet."

Grandma Scarlett was a frail old lady, and her memory had gone. Johnny decided to sell off most of the cows and kept one for their own use. He was spending money like water, and suggested to Jane that they should sell the house John had built years ago. They'd had several tenants in it, but Jane didn't want to sell it. As it was unused, Johnny decided to get rid of it, and so one night he burned it down—he said that a tramp must have broken in and dropped a match. Jane was heart-broken—and in her heart she didn't believe him.

She still had the bank account in her name, but was constantly drawing money out for Johnny. She became confused, and one day Johnny took her to the bank and asked her to sign a form. She did, and signed all the money over to him without knowing what she was doing. Finally one morning, Johnny found her dead in bed. The doctor said it was a heart attack—Eleanor even wondered if he had poisoned her— he seemed capable of doing anything.

So the lovely old farmhouse became a meeting place for Johnny's fast friends. He sold a lot of the lovely furniture and finally brought home a widow, very made up, and they drank like fishes.

Eleanor called one day with the children and found them in bed, drunk and incapable. She left holding Jessica's hand and turned back to look at the home which had been so happy, and was now so ne- glected, and quietly made her way back to Thomas.

The Scarlett Roses

In a field by a river my love and I did stand
And on my leaning shoulder he laid his manly hand,
He bid me take life easy as the grass grows on the weir,
But I was young and foolish, and now am full of tears.

WB Yeats

The Scarlett Roses

Joe Lyons had a sad life. At school his father, the headmaster, caned him daily. Joe wasn't as clever as his two sisters or his brother, but he had a lot of common sense, and a great love of nature.

One day, when he was fourteen, his father arrived home drunk. He had beaten the old horse all the seven miles from town and it had collapsed and died as Joe tried to revive it, and his father had punched Joe in the mouth and gone to bed. Joe had vowed to never enter the house again and had struggled the four miles to the Scarletts' house where Jane and John Scarlett nursed him through pneumonia, and John later found him a job as stable lad on a big estate.

He continued to visit the Scarletts and hoped to marry Anna, but Anna was a timid girl and refused him. Then three years later he asked Kathleen, the elder, to marry him and she, several years older than he was, accepted him. She was a good housewife, quite hand-some, but in his heart he still loved Anna.

He and Kathleen had a son born in 1914, and as the first world war started Joe and his brother-in-law Robert Scarlett enlisted, and by the time they got back tired, dirty, hungry and disillusioned, Joe's son Sam, four years old and totally spoiled, had slept in his mother's bed since Joe went away, and refused to sleep anywhere else. He did nothing that Joe asked him to do, and one day when they were going out, Joe said, "Sam drink your milk, we are ready to go," and Sam turned the mug of milk upside down all over the table cloth, Joe picked him up and putting him across his knee slapped his bottom, but Kathleen shouted at him to stop. "You are getting as bad as your father," she said.

After that Joe gave up. He left Sam to Kathleen and gave his mind to his job. He had never really loved Kathleen, though he had been ready to keep her happy and he loved Sam, but it was difficult to love such an obnoxious child.

So the weary years went by, Joe sleeping in the spare bedroom, and eleven year old Sam sleeping with his mother.

• • •

63

Joe wondered how long it could go on. He decided to go and speak to his father-in-law, John Scarlett.

"It won't alter until you get out of that little cottage," John said.

"Where can I go, or what can I do. I want the best for both of them."

John put his hand on Joe's shoulder. "You are a good man—think hard and you will find a solution, and Jane and I will back you all the way."

Joe went home. A few days later a letter arrived from Jane inviting them all for a week-end. Robert and Eileen and their two boys, and of course Eleanor and Thomas who lived nearby. The cousins could all get together, and the adults could exchange news.

Jane and Anna made up beds and camp beds, and soon they were all together. Jane and John loved these family round-ups, and on Saturday afternoon Robert said, "Let's all have a game of football. Joe, you in one goal and me in the other, and Thomas can be referee."

John Scarlett and John McMahon against Sam, Ed and Harold, but Sam wouldn't play—he sat on the ground hugging his knees, watching them. Ed headed a goal past Robert, who cleared it up the field. Then Harold kicked the ball, and it hit Sam.

"Kick it back," they all shouted, but Sam sat there crying.

Grandad John walked over to them at that moment. He knocked the ball to them and took Sam's hand. "Let's go for a walk," he said, wiping Sam's eyes and taking him towards the workshop.

"I want Mammie," said Sam.

"What do you want her for?"

"I want to tell that I've been hurt."

"Have you been hurt?" John asked, looking into Sam's face. "Show me where. I don't see any blood, and I can't see a bruise—are you sure you've been hurt?"

Sam didn't answer.

"Come into the workshop. I want to show you what I've just finished."

At the far end of the workshop stood a lovely oak desk, gleaming softly in the sunlight from the window. "What do you think of it?" John asked.

Sam walked over to it. He touched the dark green leather top, and then the four drawers. Each drawer had two entwined roses carved on it, and the drawer handles were like little brass vases. "How do you open them?" he asked.

John lifted a brass vase and pulled. The drawer opened smoothly.

"Did you make the roses yourself?"

"Yes," replied his grandfather, "those roses are my trade mark—they are the Scarlett Roses. Wherever you see them on any piece of furniture, you will know I made it."

"What do you call the wood?" Sam asked.

"Oak" said John.

Sam wandered around and picked up a small piece. "What's this?"

"That's oak too," John said.

"It's a different colour, and it's rough," said Sam.

John picked up a plane and ran it over the little block. "Here you try it." Sam did as John showed him. "Now look at it—it is smooth—then it would be stained and varnished and polished.

"Can I keep this bit?"

"Of course, you have just made it." The grandfather smiled. Sam wasn't such a bad boy after all. "Your father was telling me about the Shetland ponies. Do you like them?"

"I haven't seen them," Sam replied

"Why not?" John was surprised.

"Mammie doesn't like me going near the horses. I'd like to see them."

"Well, next time your father is going up there at the week-ends, ask him if you can come with him. He won't let anything happen to you.

Kathleen met them as they got back to the house. "I've been worried about you, you have been so long. The others have been back for ages. I hope you haven't caught cold, Sam."

Sam held up his block. "Look what I made," he said, "Grandad is so clever—he makes roses and lovely things. I want to work with him when I grow up."

The following week-end when Joe was going up to the stables, Sam said, "Can I come with you, Daddy?"

Kathleen stiffened. "I don't think that's a good idea," she said.

Joe looked hard at her. "I think its a great idea. I haven't had a walk with my son for years."

"Well mind he keeps well back from them."

Joe laughed. "The two little girls from the Castle are four and six years old, and they groom them and ride them—he will come to no harm, have no fear."

Sam held Joe's hand, when they came to the field. Sam couldn't believe his eyes—the pretty little horses all came to the gate and jostled each other for Joe's attention. He put his hand in his pocket and brought out some cube sugar. "Feed them with that," he said.

Sam wasn't sure. "Will they bite my fingers?"

"Not if you hold the sugar on the palm of your hand—mind it will tickle a bit."

Sam laughed as the little horses ate from his hand.

Joe popped a sugar cube into Sam's mouth as they walked home. Sam was like a new boy—he didn't whinge or cry, and even Kathleen had to admit to herself that the outing had done him good.

• • •

Lady Archdale became famous for her little horses. She was a superb horsewoman and rode with the hounds, entered her Shetlands in Agricultural shows, and the children won rosettes and cups galore. She had a little carriage made, and the children drove it harnessed to their two matching ponies. People flocked to the shows to see them.

Joe was always on hand and he did well financially, for whenever there were prizes won, Joe was tipped handsomely. He had been saving all his working life. Kathleen had money too, and she was a good housekeeper like her mother. She wasted nothing, she made Sam's clothes until he was ten years old, and she made her own. She also knitted jumpers for them all as well as socks. Joe wanted to get back into his own bed. Sam would, he believed, have swapped beds with him, but Kathleen changed the subject whenever Joe even hinted.

He was getting discontented with his life, and wasn't sure what he wanted. He envied Thomas and Eleanor, and thought their children were a credit to them—the boys were real boys and Polly so pretty and well behaved, and their new little son Bob. Joe knew that his own life was far more comfortable than theirs, but he would have changed places with them for children like they had.

• • •

Eleanor would never have guessed that anyone could envy her. It was Monday, and wash day. Thomas had carried several buckets of water for her, but she needed more and he was working in the fields with his father. She and Jeannie had had a terrible row on Sunday, and Jeannie had gone out. Polly aged four and a half and Bob aged three were playing on the doorstep—she couldn't leave them alone, so she strapped Bob into the pram and stood Polly in a tea chest. She had used the tea chest for all the children—it wasn't ideal, but they had to stay in it whether they cried or not. At least they were safe until she got back from the stream. She was pregnant again, and this time she wasn't happy. Her back ached, she was tired, and she felt she could have slept for a month.

Just as she picked the buckets up a voice said, "I'll get the water, you put the kettle on."

It was Anna her sister. "Eleanor, you are worn out," Anna said as they drank their tea. "I'll tell you what—get Polly and Bob ready and I'll take them home for a few days. Mother and Father would love to have them."

Eleanor could have cried with relief—only the two boys at school to see to.

John and Jane were delighted to have the children. They both worried about Eleanor, just as they worried about Kathleen. There was no doubt that Thomas and Eleanor loved each other and the children, but they were so poor. John always gave them money for Christmas, and it helped, but Thomas was proud—he didn't like charity.

Eleanor and Anna often talked about Kathleen. "You should have married him Anna," Eleanor said, "I used to watch him watching you—you froze him out,"

"I know," Anna signed, "I hated hurting him—he was a really nice lad, but at that time I was terrified of sex and childbirth."

"What about now?"

"I'm still a bit scared, but you made it look easy. I worry about my future. Mother and Father won't live forever, and Johnny will get the farm and everything. What will happen to me if he brings home one of those trollops he spends his time and money on?"

"You could come and live with us."

Anna laughed. "If you go on having babies you will need to build an extension on the house—and can you picture, you and me against Jeannie?" They both laughed at that.

Bob and Polly stayed with their grandparents until the baby arrived—a little girl this time—and Anna came for a fortnight and made Eleanor stay in bed. She was glad to—bone tired and glad it was over.

When the baby was three weeks old, Eleanor and Thomas and all the children went down to the Scarletts. Eleanor handed the new baby to her father, and he loved her—her thatch of dark hair and tiny features and great navy blue eyes reminded him of Eleanor, who was his favourite child, and he knew this one would be his favourite grandchild. She put up a tiny hand and grasped his beard. He laughed and said, "Call her Jessica—she's a smart baby."

Joe woke up early on Sunday morning. On weekdays he started work at five thirty, and on Sundays he still woke up early.

He lay quietly for a while and thought about his talk with John Scarlett. John couldn't advise him, and felt in his heart that as long as they lived in the two bedroom cottage at Archdale things wouldn't change. Sam, now eleven years old, still slept with Kathleen and Joe slept in the spare room, growing more lonely as the years went by. He got up and dressed, went quietly down stairs, lit the fire and put on the kettle. While he waited for it to boil, he went to the shed and got out his bicycle. He didn't ride it much these days, but still found it in good order. Indoors again, he made a pot of tea, boiled a couple of eggs and buttered some bread. Once upon a time he would have taken a cup of tea up to Kathleen. He had done that a year or so ago, but the sight of Sam's head on Kathleen's shoulder irritated him, and he didn't go in there again.

He rode his bicycle along the lovely country lanes. He wasn't sure what he was looking for, and after an hour he sat down on the grass to rest opposite a pair of cottages. One had curtains and a tidy garden, but the other one seemed empty, the garden over grown and the path weedy. He sat there wondering who had lived there, and presently a man came along driving three cows.

They said "Good morning," as country folks do, and Joe asked him who owned the empty cottage.

"I do," replied the man. "I lived there till my father died and then we moved into the farmhouse."

"Who lives in the other one?"

"That's my sister—she is a war widow. Why do you ask?"

"I wondered if the empty one was for sale," Joe said. "But I would need to lease a bit of ground as well if I bought it."

"Come on up to the house," the man said. "Perhaps we can help each other."

Joe told them he had been a groom at Archdale for more than twenty years—he wanted to start a market garden and be his own boss, he said, and asked how much the farmer wanted for the cottage.

"A hundred and seventy five pounds," he was told.

Joe knew he could manage that, and asked if he could have the key and look around. There was a nice front room and a kitchen and scullery down stairs, with a built-in dresser and a range in the kitchen. Upstairs there was a front bedroom and one looking out the back, and a small room over the scullery. Although it had been empty, he couldn't see any sign of damp. The windows were quite big for a cottage, and the front rooms would get the afternoon sun. He liked it.

When he returned the key, the man said he could rent the field next to the cottage for ten pound per year if he was thinking of buying, admitting he could do with the money, as they were having a job to survive after the death of his parents.

Joe said he would be back next Sunday, and rode home happily. He had decided to buy—he had also decided not to tell Kathleen, but they were going to move whether she liked it or not. He didn't want her to start nagging him just yet.

So the sale was completed, and the farmer, glad to get the money, offered to plough the field for him. Joe stole away every Sunday and cleared the ground. He felt guilty—he hadn't been to church for weeks and he had never laboured on Sunday, but he hoped God would forgive him.

After two months he gave notice at Archdale. Lady Archdale was very sorry to lose him and couldn't understand why he was leaving. He told her he still loved the horses, but his personal life was in a muddle and this was the only way he could sort it out.

Two weeks later he told Kathleen to start packing. They would be moving in two weeks.

"Where to?" she wanted to know, but he just replied, "You'll see when we get there."

Kathleen arranged a meeting with Her Ladyship and asked her if Joe had been sacked.

Good Heavens no, she was told, we are all sorry to lose him, he didn't ask for references but he would get a good one anyway. He must have his own reasons, but perhaps you know more about that than I do.

Joe bought wallpaper and linoleum and a bed-side mat for the little bedroom. He also bought a single bed and a chest of drawers, he even bought blankets, sheets and pillows, and he was pleased with the result. It was a lovely little room, just right for a twelve year old boy.

Old Peter Monk was sorry to see them go. Joe had been his right hand man for years. No-one knew where they were going, as Joe had told no-one. He was given a golden hand shake from the Archdales, the van arrived and picked up their belongings, and they arrived at the cottage.

"I'll show you your room Sam," said Joe, and took him up. Kathleen followed. "I haven't done anything to your room, Kathleen—no doubt you will want to decorate it yourself. This is Sam's bedroom, and the front one is yours."

Kathleen turned. "If you think you are coming into my room, Joe, you are mistaken."

Joe looked at her with hard eyes. "I wouldn't dream of coming into your room—that bedroom is mine, that one is yours, and this one is Sam's—and if I catch him sneaking into your bed at any time I'll break every bone in his body."

"How are we going to live no wages coming in?"

"You can get your sewing machine going and I'll get the garden going. By next year we should be making a living. I intend to open a market garden, and I've asked your father to build a couple of greenhouses. I will have plenty to sell and enough for ourselves, and what we don't have we will do without."

The market garden took off. Joe could sell everything he could grow, and more. Kathleen having sulked for a while asked Joe, if she made bread and cakes did he think they would sell. "Try it," he said, "if it doesn't sell we can eat it ourselves." But every Saturday Kathleen's stall was sold out with orders for next week.

They didn't argue—Joe wasn't a spiteful man, but he didn't want to sleep with Kathleen. He was dog tired every night, although Kathleen sometimes came out and helped in the garden.

One night he thought he heard a step on the landing. He went out and Kathleen had her hand on Sam's bedroom door.

She jumped when Joe came out of his room. "I wanted to see if he was alright," she said.

"Go back to bed," said Joe, "he is fast asleep and so should you be."

"I'll just take a look," she pleaded.

"No, Kathleen. God forgive me but I'll slap you in a minute—go back to your bed.

Kathleen wondered what had happened to Joe, always so gentle and kind—she never did see that she had made him like this.

Before they moved, Joe had gone down to the school. It was only a ten minute walk from the cottage. He saw the headmaster, told him he had bought Yew Cottage and that he would like Sam to start—so on the following Monday, Kathleen started to put her coat on to walk to school with him. Joe told her to take it off. The teacher knew Sam was coming, and the children from the farm were going to call for him on his first day. "We don't want them to think that he's a mammies boy, do we?" he added slyly.

70

Kathleen felt like running away, but where to? Joe had taken things into his own hands and really she couldn't find fault.

Their neighbour Mrs Molly Peters was in her forties. She was a good looking woman, tall, slim, chestnut hair and hazel eyes. She used to lean over the fence and talk to Joe, and Kathleen often heard them laughing together. Mrs Peters had a daughter a bit younger than Sam, and they walked home from school together. Kathleen felt shut out— she didn't seem to have anyone to relax with.

The farmer's wife was friendly and when Kathleen went to fetch the milk they chatted, but she was a busy lady as she and her husband did all the work between them. Kathleen offered to help, and was hurt when told, "We can't afford paid help."

"I don't want to be paid," she said, "I'm always there if you need me."

The woman smiled and patted her arm. "I'll remember that," she said, "we all need each other, sooner or later."

Molly Peters was a mystery to Kathleen. She wore long flimsy dresses, mostly green or yellow with a gold belt, was always barefooted, and usually her auburn hair hung loose to her waist. She wasn't idle by any means, and when Kathleen opened her curtains at six o'clock in the morning she would see Molly working in her vegetable garden, where she grew masses of vegetables and salads.

She seemed to wash her hair nearly every day, and worked in the garden while it dried. Her daughter Cassie had the same colouring, with freckled face and arms and beautiful green eyes. Kathleen asked the farmer's wife about her. "Oh, Molly is a free spirit," she answered, "her husband was training to be a doctor but dropped out and joined the navy and was lost at sea. Molly is a trained nurse and midwife—she delivers most of the babies around here. She would dearly love to work at the hospital, but they don't employ married women. But she manages. She comes in and helps with the hay-making and harvesting, and she's a great cook."

Sam was fascinated by Cassie. She was very lively, and she could play football like a boy. She was also learning music and had lessons from Mrs Stewart, the schoolmaster's wife. Molly had a piano in the cottage, and Kathleen sometimes heard Molly play it when Cassie was at school.

One day, Sam asked Kathleen if he could have music lessons.

"We haven't got a piano for you to practise on."

"But I can practise on Cassie's—Mrs Peters said I could."

"I don't want you to be a nuisance," said Kathleen.

A few days later Molly knocked at the door. "Can I have a word, Mrs Lyons?"

"Of course, come in," Kathleen said, "I'm just going to have a cup of tea—you can join me."

Over tea Molly said, "Sam would like piano lessons—he can practise on my piano, it would be no trouble. He's a nice boy—I'm glad Cassie and him get on so well. She used to be a bit lonely."

"What about the three children at the farm?" Kathleen asked.

"They are a bit older and they have to work—they have all got their jobs to do. My sister-in-law is quite strict with them. They come down sometimes, but my brother and his wife think I'm too soft with Cassie. I make her keep her room tidy and wash up, but there isn't much for a child to do in a little house like mine."

So it was arranged. Sam was going to have music lessons with Mrs Stewart for one hour every Saturday morning. He insisted on going alone, which was just as well as Kathleen had her cake stall on Saturdays.

• • •

Sam knocked and Mrs Stewart opened the door.

"Hello Sam. Come into the sitting room—I'll be with you in a minute."

He went in and looked all around after she left him. It was a nice room—the piano stood against the far wall, two large chairs one each side of the fire and a chaise-longue under the window. A lovely glass-fronted cabinet stood behind the door, full of china, teapots, cups and saucers, nice glasses and a few ornaments. Sam looked up—on the curved top were two entwined roses. He laughed out loud.

When Mrs Stewart came back in, he pointed to the cabinet and said excitedly, "My Grandad made that."

"Made what?" she asked.

"Your lovely cupboard. Those roses up there are his trade-mark."

"Are you sure?"

"Quite sure."

"Well then, your Grandad must be John Scarlett. My father had that cabinet made for us when we got married. But your name is Lyons."

"My mother was Kathleen Scarlett," replied Sam.

Joe wondered how long it would be before Sam got fed up with the piano, but he stayed with it and enjoyed going round next door to practise.

John and Jane Scarlett came to see the cottage and the garden. John was pleased that it was going well—he and Joe spent a long time debating about the size of the greenhouses and deciding the best position.

"What sort of wood do you think?" Joe asked.

"Oh cedar," said John. "It's a bit more expensive, but varnish it and it will last for years."

John measured up and told Joe what to order. "Let me know when it arrives and I'll come down with the men and it will be up in no time,"

"There's the glass as well," said Joe.

"Leave that for now. I know just the man to do it. He'll know what's needed when the woodwork is done."

Jane and Kathleen went over the house together. Jane thought it was lovely. "Sam's room is nice," she said, "and you have a spare room now."

Kathleen didn't answer—how could she tell her mother that Joe still slept in the spare room. But Joe told John quite bluntly—he was glad to have got Sam out of Kathleen's bed, but he was happy the way things were.

As they walked back to the cottage, Molly Peters was standing on a chair by the apple tree, barefooted as usual. She was stretching up into the apple tree, and the brisk wind made her flimsy green dress billow out behind her, showing the shape of her splendid bosom and slim hips. Her hair flowed out in the wind like a flame.

"Who is that?" asked John.

"That's our neighbour, Mrs Peters," Joe replied.

"She is very unusual," John said.

"She is very beautiful," Joe said quietly.

As they sat down to tea, Jane also asked about the neighbour. "I saw her from the upstairs window," she said

"That is Molly Peters," replied Kathleen. "Her daughter Cassie is the same age as Sam, and they are great friends."

Sam arrived home from school then and Cassie followed him in. He greeted his grand parents and introduced her to them.

"Mrs Stewart wants us to play a duet at the Christmas party," he said, "so we will be going out the same time on Saturdays from now on."

John and Jane were pleased with Sam. He was big for his age and didn't hang round Kathleen any more. But as the children went out again Kathleen said, "It's always Cassie these days, Cassie said this or

Cassie's done that. She is all he thinks about. He spends more time next door than he does at home."

Jane thought, Kathleen is jealous her little baby is growing up and she doesn't like it. "What is her real name," she asked.

"Sam tells me it's Cassandra," replied Kathleen. "I've never heard of it before."

"Well, it is unusual," Jane said, "but it's a pretty name."

"Any chance of you coming up for a week-end?" Jane said.

Joe shook his head. "I really won't be able to get away, but Kathleen and Sam could go. I'll manage to feed myself for a day or two."

"What about my cake stall on Saturday morning?" asked Kathleen.

"Well you can get it all ready on Friday morning and catch the afternoon train, Sam can have the afternoon off from school, and I can sell your cakes. Most of them are orders now."

"I'll think about it," Kathleen said.

So on Friday, Kathleen and Sam went off and promised to come back Monday morning. Joe quite enjoyed having the house to himself. On Friday evening, he could hear Cassie on the piano, running up and down the scales. Then later he heard a lovely old Irish ballad and he found himself singing along, "O Danny Boy, the pipes, the pipes are calling." It was being played softly and he felt his eyes filling with tears—he didn't know why.

Next morning he was up at five thirty filling his stall, and had cut cauliflowers, cabbages and lettuce, spring onion, carrots and parsnips. He wished he had enough ground for potatoes, but he knew they were for sale at all the farms. The townspeople came out in droves on bicycles, on foot and some in cars. He put up Kathleen's stall, and heard a voice, "Do you need any help?"

It was Molly, still barefooted but her hair piled high.

"I think I can manage," he said.

"I'll do the cakes." Molly said. "I've put a stew on, we can eat it when we finish. Cassie has just left to stay with friends until tomorrow night—I don't like eating alone Joe, so please come and keep me company."

They were busy for a couple of hours and everything was sold. "Not a bad mornings work," said Molly.

"It was great," said Joe, "my best so far." They tidied up and counted the money—nearly ten pounds. "I worked a month for that at the stud."

"Well you've put in a good few hours growing them, its not all profit," she replied.

They sat down to eat in the kitchen, which was like Molly: yellow and white table cloth, and crockery, a dresser full of yellow and white china, the range was polished and everything was very clean but a bit untidy.

"I should have changed my clothes before coming round," said Joe.

She laughed. "I like things casual. I haven't put my shoes on either."

Joe helped to clear the table, and did the wiping up. He reached around her to put away the cutlery and found his arms about her. Her hair smelt of ripe strawberries and he buried his face in its sweetness. They kissed slowly, and then she moved away.

"I didn't intend that to happen," she said.

"Neither did I," said Joe, "but I've wanted to do it since I first saw you."

"Me too," she said, "but it must stop there—Kathleen will be back, and Cassie and Sam. We must be sensible—too many people will get hurt, nice people who don't deserve to be hurt."

Joe walked slowly to the door. "I'm sorry Molly, honestly I am."

She ran to him, her eyes full of tears. "Dear Joe, don't be sorry. I loved it, I really did." She hugged him and they kissed again.

Joe went out and walked home. He had work to do in his garden, but he sat remembering her sweetness. She was lovely, and Joe was falling in love—and there was nothing in the world he could do about it.

At last he went out to the garden. He worked steadily until seven thirty, then went indoors, stripped off and washed and shaved. He should have something to eat, but he didn't feel hungry, so he drank several cups of tea and finally went to bed at ten o'clock. Normally he fell asleep quickly, but tonight he tossed and turned. He looked at the clock—12 o'clock—he turned and closed his eyes, but all he could think of was Molly's bright hair and soft mouth. He groaned and turned over. One thirty, still no sleep. He got up and pulled his trousers on. It was chilly. He pulled on a jumper, went downstairs and out through the back door. He sat down on the little bench—there was silence all round except for little animal rustlings in the hedge, Then he heard a different sound and looked round. Molly stood there in her white nightgown.

"Molly, you will catch your death of cold," he whispered.

"I can't sleep."

"Neither can I."

"Come over here then," she said.

He stepped over the fence, and she took his hand and led him through the back door and up the stairs. He followed as if he was sleep walking. Molly pulled off her nightgown and got into bed. She held out her arms. He undressed and went to her. They made love slowly, as though they weren't in control, then lay in each others arms and fell asleep.

Joe woke at five o'clock. He couldn't remember where he was, then suddenly they were back in each others arms again. He crept out and into his own house at six thirty, feeling so happy he almost danced for joy. This lovely woman loved him—whatever happened in the future, he loved and was loved. He had never felt like this about Kathleen, but he had stayed true to her until now. He knew she would be back, and things would go the same way they always had.

He hardly knew Molly. Nothing about her life or her late husband. Had she loved him? Not like this, he thought—no one had ever loved like this. He walked round his garden—no work today only the bare essentials. He dressed in his suit and went to church, praying for guidance and joining in the singing. As he came out he saw a tall figure in front of him. He didn't recognise the dark costume, hat, stockings and shoes, but when she turned he saw it was Molly. She waited, smiling.

"Good morning Joe."

"I didn't recognise you."

"I expect it was the shoes that put you off. I don't wear shoes except to Church."

"Well I learn a bit more about you every day," he said, and they both laughed.

They talked of general things and caught up with Molly's brother and sister-in-law and their children. They all walked home together, and Joe began to wonder if he had dreamt last night, they were both so calm—but as he turned into his gate, she smiled her lovely smile and said, "Thanks Joe."

• • •

The rest of Sunday, Joe and Molly didn't see each other. He made sure that the house was clean and tidy, went for a long walk and got home at nine thirty. Then he went to bed and slept soundly all night, getting up at his usual time of five thirty. He lit his fire, boiled the kettle, and drank his cup of tea. When he went out, he saw Molly working in her garden.

"Hello Molly."

She waved back, "Morning Joe." They both carried on working.

At twelve o'clock Kathleen and Sam arrived home. Joe put his arms around Sam.

"Welcome home son, have you had a good week-end?"

"I've been playing with John and Harold McMahon—we went fishing and played football."

"Did you catch a fish then?"

"Only a tiny one—we threw it back into the water—is Cassie in?"

"I don't know, I expect she's at school," said Joe. Then to Kathleen, "How are your family?"

"They seem alright," she replied. "Dad said he and the men will be down on Wednesday. Has the wood arrived yet?"

"Yes it came this morning—there seems to be an awful lot of it, but your father knows what he is doing."

"I didn't see much of Johnny," she said, "he doesn't do much on the farm—Mother has to work hard."

"What about Anna—isn't she pulling her weight?" asked Joe.

"Ah now there's a question—she may be getting married."

Joe looked amazed. "Who to?"

"Well, do you remember George Grant at school? Maybe you remember him getting married about ten years ago. Well anyhow, his wife died a year ago—he has two small boys and he is calling on Anna."

"Where does he live?"

"Newtownbutler, on the Crom Castle side. He has a small farm there. I don't think he has much money, but Anna has a good bit salted down, and I think she likes him."

"She said she would never marry."

"Well I think she is using her head now. When Mam and Dad are gone she won't have much of a life with Johnny and his loose women. Besides, she must be thirty five or thirty six now, and she wont have a child—that's what frightens her," said Kathleen. Then she asked, "How did the stalls go on Saturday?"

"Great," said Joe, "nine pounds seventeen shillings and sixpence."

"You were busy, then?"

"Mrs Peters came round and did the cake stall, and she gave me dinner," Joe said.

77

"How kind of her," said Kathleen, "they are nice, her and Cassie. Sam was telling everyone about Cassie and about them doing the duet at Christmas. I felt proud of him. He got on with Eleanor's boys, and I hardly saw him at all."

"That's good," Joe agreed, "we don't bring our children up for ourselves—we have to lose them sooner or later to someone else."

"Oh but not just yet," Kathleen said, "he is only twelve."

"I am going to ask him to help in the gardens—I will give him a little pay packet if he works well," said Joe.

• • •

Anna got married on the Wednesday before Christmas. It was a small family wedding—neither Anna or George wanted a big do. George's two sisters and their husbands were there, and Robert and Eileen, Eleanor and Thomas, and Joe, Kathleen and Sam. Jane and John paid some local ladies to come in to prepare the food, and it was very well done.

Joe left before the reception was over—he had to get back to his gardens and greenhouses. There was frost in the air, and he had to light heaters and cover shrubs. He was selling flowers and shrubs. His market garden went from strength to strength—he couldn't grow enough to satisfy all his customers, and he had put out a feeler with the farmer hoping to get another field. The farmer didn't say yes—he didn't say no either, but Joe didn't think he would let him have more land.

Thomas and Eleanor and their two youngest had paid a surprise visit in the autumn. Thomas was impressed.

"My God, Joe," he said, "I'd kill for a garden like this."

Joe smiled. "But you have a farm—you could have a market garden of your own."

"Why don't you take some cuttings of those roses in the back?" Thomas suggested.

"I'm not sure I'd know how," said Joe.

"I'll show you."

They worked away, Joe preparing pots of compost and Thomas with his penknife out, carefully cutting the strong shoots.

Molly, watching from her kitchen window, was curious and unable to stand it any longer she came out.

Thomas looked up: "Hello," he said.

"I've been wondering what you are doing. I'm Molly Peters, Joe and Kathleen's neighbour."

"Have you never planted rose cuttings?" Thomas asked.

"No. I've tried, but I can't have done it right, they always die. These are lovely roses, I don't know their names—I'm sure they have names."

"You have some nice ones over there too."

"Well, you show me how and I'll try it," Molly said.

Joe arrived with a barrow full of pots of compost. "I see you two have met," he said. "If these grow I'll make a bit of money on them."

Kathleen and Eleanor came out and walked over to them. The three heads were close together, Molly in the middle, her hair flowing over Joe's and Thomas's shoulders. The sight disturbed Kathleen— she never got this close to Joe or Thomas. Eleanor wasn't bothered by it—she carried her little son Bill in her arms, and Jessica held her hand. Molly turned and smiled at them.

"This is my little sister Eleanor, and Jessica and Bill," Kathleen said.

Molly shook hands with Eleanor, kissed the top of Jessica's head, and held her arms out for the baby. "It's a long time since I held one this size," she said. Bill was fifteen months old and a big child.

"I hear you are a midwife," said Eleanor.

"Yes, I help out when I'm needed," replied Molly. "It was my favourite part of nursing—new life and happy parents, what could be better?" Then she took Jessica's hand: "I've got something to show you," she said, "come with me." She picked Jessica up and stepped over the fence.

"You've no shoes on," Jessica said.

"No," said Molly, "I like running barefoot."

"So do I," said Jessica, "I like paddling in the stream—have you got a stream?"

"No, I wish I had," Molly said.

They went through to Molly's sitting room. In a glass case sat the tiniest little carriage and horses Jessica had ever seen. Molly lifted it out onto the table. It was the thinnest china—the little coachman could be taken out and the little door had a hinge. Molly lifted out two tiny ladies, one dressed in blue and one in pink. One held a little parasol which opened, and their shoes came off. She unharnessed the horses and let Jessica hold one in her hand. Jessica was speechless.

"Aren't they beautiful?" Molly asked.

"Lovely," breathed Jessica.

"My great grandmother gave them to my grandmother," said Molly, "and she gave them to my mother. My mother gave them to me and I will give them to my daughter."

"I hope she doesn't break them," Jessica said.

Molly looked in her cake tin and found a slice of chocolate cake—she tied a towel around Jessica's neck to keep her dress clean—and when she had eaten it, Molly took her back to Kathleen.

"Have you seen Mrs Peters little coach?" Jessica asked Kathleen.

"No I haven't—you must be very special—she doesn't show it to everyone."

At that, Jessica felt very important.

• • •

Joe was using the back garden of his cottage as well as the field, and was working with the roses. One day when a last, beautiful, pale yellow rose was in bud, Molly came to the fence.

"That's a beautiful rose," she said.

He smiled at her, picked the rose and handed to her. She shook her head laughing. Joe stuck the rose in her hair—it looked lovely. Kathleen at the kitchen window saw it all, and she suddenly realised why Joe was so happy these days—he was carrying on with Molly, but when? Perhaps she was reading too much into a gesture that was typical of Joe.

She didn't mention it when Joe came in. He had picked a bunch of Chrysanthemums for her, bronze and yellow—she blushed with pleasure, but Joe knew she had seen, and he knew he would have to be careful and try to not show his feelings.

Then March the telegram came—John Scarlett had died. Both Joe and Kathleen were numb with shock, and Sam wept. They all came home for the funeral—Molly and Cassie begged Sam to stay with them, but he wanted to go. Molly said not to worry about the garden as she would see to everything.

• • •

Jessica had been two years old when Grandad Scarlett had woken one morning and couldn't dress because his left hand and arm just wouldn't work. Jane, alarmed, sent for the doctor. He said John had had a slight stroke, gave him some tablets, and assured him that the feeling would return. And it did—not completely, but he could do most things. He spent more time then with his grandchildren and less time in his work shop.

Just after Jessica's fourth birthday he had another stroke, and this time he died.

Jessica missed him very much—he had been so warm, his great arms were a haven against anything that threatened her, and poor Jane, his wife, was left staring into an empty void. She didn't know how to face each new day—they had loved each other from first till last.

Jane sat at her dressing table brushing her hair—little Jessica knocked and came in.

"Gran, let me brush your hair," she said.

Jane smiled a wan smile. "Alright dear, you can brush it for a while."

Jessica climbed on to a chair and brushed the long hair. She looked at their reflections in the mirror, then she said, "Those two roses on the top of your mirror are like you and Grandad. You were always together like them. Do you think one of them will die now too—they are the Scarlett Roses."

Jane couldn't answer. This four year old understood more than her own children. She gathered her hair and dressed it, then went out through the orchard and sat down under an apple tree and cried till she had no tears left.

It was the biggest funeral ever seen in St Mary's Church, Drummully. Eleanor, Anna and Kathleen prepared food, and Jane watched them. She looked ill and lost. People shook her hand and offered condolences—she was like a clockwork doll, shaking hands and saying thank you.

Kathleen said to Joe after the funeral, "I feel as eldest daughter that I should stay with mother for a few weeks. Sam can stay with me. It's almost Easter and he will be home from school anyway."

So Joe went back alone. John Scarlett had been his friend and adviser for years, and he knew he would miss him more than Kathleen did.

Molly had taken care of everything. She stood in his kitchen and put her arms around him—then she laid her head against him and he stroked her hair. They kissed without passion, almost like an old married couple.

"I've missed you," she said. "I like seeing you move around the field. If you are not there I'm unhappy."

"I miss you too—we never get a chance to touch, but I like seeing you too," Joe told her. "Where is Cassie?"

"I think she has gone to the farm—she misses Sam."

"Can I come round to you when she's asleep?" Joe asked.

"I'll come round to you when she's asleep," Molly replied.

They kissed again.

During the three weeks that Kathleen was away, Molly came round several times. Even with Kathleen away they had to be careful—the farmer or his wife would often drop into either cottage for a chat. When they were together they made love and just talked. It had never been a passionate affair—just being together was enough.

On the Thursday after Joe came back, Molly asked him what was going to happen to Kathleen's bread stall on Saturday.

He scratched his head: "I'm afraid I'll have to forget that."

"I could do it," Molly said. "I bake quite well—it would keep it going until Kathleen comes back. If it's not there, her customers will drift off and find some place else to buy their bread and cake."

Joe thought for a minute. "Alright," he said, "if you take and keep whatever money you make, its a bargain."

So Molly baked and sold her wares, just as Kathleen did. No-one noticed the difference, and the orders for next week were the same. After they had sold out, the farmer and his wife came into Joe's kitchen.

"Just in time for a cup of tea," Joe said. "Give Molly a shout—she deserves one too," and the four of them sat round the table.

"I have a lot of eggs and I make butter as you know," the farmer's wife said. "We wondered, would you mind me having a stall as well? I wouldn't bake—I haven't got time in any case—but I often have chickens as well, and Fred often shoots more rabbits than we need."

Then the farmer added, "If you are agreeable, you can have half of that field behind the cottages—I'll give it to you free. After all, you started all this—your Saturday market is known far and wide."

Joe couldn't see any reason to refuse. "I'm going to need some help," he said.

"Look no further," Molly laughed, "take me on as paid help and I'll show you I can work as hard as any man."

"I know you can," Joe smiled, "your vegetable garden is living proof."

"What about Kathleen?" Molly asked. "Do you think she'll mind us making all these decisions in her absence?"

"She'll still have her stall—you won't have time to bake and she wouldn't want you to," Joe replied. "It'll be alright, you'll see."

• • •

Joe and Kathleen were finishing their evening meal. Sam had eaten his quickly and gone up to his room—he reappeared shortly with his football boots in his hand.

"Where are you going?" Kathleen asked.

"We're having a friendly match on the school playing fields," he said.

"Put your coat on," she said.

"I don't need it, it's not cold."

"Put your coat on at once." Kathleen had raised her voice.

Sam looked at her, his eyes blazing. "I don't need a bloody coat—I told you it's not cold," he shouted, and slammed the door behind him.

Kathleen's face was bright red. Joe carried on reading his paper.

"You shouldn't let him speak to me like that," she blazed.

Joe looked up at her. "He didn't swear at me," he said. "When he does I'll deal with him. Whenever I've corrected him in the past, you always jumped in and sided with him. You must deal with him in your own way."

"I bought that coat for him two months ago, and it has never been on his back," Kathleen grumbled.

"Well," said Joe, "it's a pity you wasted your money. The way he is shooting up at the moment it won't fit him next winter anyway. I expect Eleanor would be glad of it for one of her brood—they don't get much."

"I have a parcel of his stuff to take to her next time I go up to see Mother. Molly gave me a bag full of clothes for Polly as well. I may go up next week—I'll go on Monday and I'll be back on Wednesday to start baking. Molly has some funny ideas," Kathleen went on. "We were talking about Eleanor's children, and she thinks Jessica is prettier than Polly. I have always thought she was such a plain little thing."

"Well your father would have agreed with her about that—he always said Jessica was a smart child."

"Smart maybe," said Kathleen, "but I'll never call her pretty."

"Well," said Joe going back to his paper, "she might fool us all and grow into a beauty—she certainly has beautiful eyes and dimples."

He's agreeing with Molly, Kathleen thought, just as Sam agrees with everything Cassie says.

When Kathleen came back from her mother's, she was surprised to find Molly working for Joe and the farm stall next to her own on Saturday. "Couldn't you have waited until I got back?" she said to Joe.

"What possible difference could it make? I know what I'm doing. You have quite a good life, Kathleen—I could use your help in the gardens, but you don't offer to help, you don't encourage Sam to help either, you really are becoming rather selfish. I'm working for us all— any help would be welcome.

So Kathleen began helping in the greenhouses. She learned easily, and Joe was free to work on his new field. Sam, now thirteen, helped too, especially early on Saturday mornings wheeling barrow loads of vegetables to the stalls. Cassie helped him—they were still great friends and still took piano lessons together.

• • •

Molly was in her sitting room. She picked up the letter and read it once again. It was from her father-in-law who lived in Surrey, England. He wanted Cassie to come and live with him and his wife and attend a school for Naval children. He offered to pay Molly's and Cassie's fare over to England—they could see the school, she could live at Hindhead and catch the bus, morning and afternoon. He hoped Molly would think it over—he said it would mean a great deal to him and his wife. They had never seen Cassie—Molly sent them a photo on her birthday each year, and they sent Cassie ten pounds at Christmas and again on her birthday.

Molly's first instinct was to say, No No No—don't take my lovely child away from me. But the more she thought about it, she began to see how reasonable it was. She would let Cassie read the letter. Cassie wrote to her grand parents quite often—whatever Cassie decided, Molly would go along with it.

She told Joe about it. Strangely, though they had often talked, Molly had never mentioned her husband or in-laws to him. Now it all poured out while they were working together in the new field. They sat down, and Molly told him how she had trained at the Adelaide Hospital, Dublin. Teddy Peters was a medical student at Trinity College. There were several students working on the wards, but Teddy was outstanding—his blond hair and green eyes made him a favourite with all the young nurses. One day Molly was coming off duty—she had been working for ten hours—and on her way across to the nurses quarters she met Teddy.

"You look all in," he had said.

"I am," she'd replied. "I don't know if my feet will get me as far as my bed."

"I'll carry you," he'd said smiling.

"When are you off duty?" she'd said. "I've a whole day off to-morrow and I go on night duty the following night."

"I'm free tomorrow afternoon. Would you care for a walk?"

They'd agreed to meet.

Next day they'd taken the trolley-bus out to Killiney. It was beautiful. They'd walked and talked—he told her his father had worked with the Embassy in Dublin, but was now in London—he was an only child, and his parents had bought a house in Surrey.

"Why did you come to Trinity?" she'd asked.

"Because it's the best" he'd replied.

Molly had completed her four years and was going on to do mid-wifery. She could still live in the nurses home, but would be working the district with the district nurse.

After that they'd met regularly, and in nineteen thirteen he'd asked her to marry him. It would have to be secretly, as he hadn't finished his training and she, as a nurse, would have to give up—married women weren't allowed to work in hospitals. She'd said no. It was difficult, but she knew both of their careers were at stake.

Then in the autumn he'd told her he had joined the Navy. There was a war coming, and please would she marry him? They were married by Special Licence, and spent two days and two nights together. His parents were furious with him—she wore her wedding ring on a string around her neck for six months. When Teddy came home on leave, he found lodgings for them and they had seven days together. Then he went away—the war had started, and three months later Molly found herself pregnant. She left the hospital and came home. Her parents were angry too. What had she done?

She never saw Teddy again—his ship went down in the Channel and the war office gave her a small pension. When the cottage became vacant, she asked her father if she could live in it, and he had given it to her. Cassie was born, Molly's parents died within six months of each other, Fred and his wife moved to the farm, and here she was.

"I've slept oftener with you, Joe, than I did with Teddy," she said.

"Did you love him?" Joe asked.

"Yes" she said, "everyone loved Teddy, he inspired love."

"I mean real love," Joe insisted.

"Joe I love you, I can't imagine my life without you, is that what you want to hear."

"Yes if you really mean it," Joe said.

"I mean it," she answered.

Molly gave her father-in-law's letter to Cassie when she came home from school. Cassie read it through.

"What do you want me to do?" she asked.

Molly said, "It's your decision and its your life—think about the pro's and con's—we'll talk tonight."

After their evening meal Cassie began, "I only want to do whatever you want. Mam. We have been such good friends. If I go will you be lonely—you know you hate eating on your own."

Molly stopped her. "Listen my darling," she said, "from the day you were born I've always known that one day you would go and live your own way. This is a terrific opportunity for you—you will get a good education, you will learn sports like tennis and hockey, you will get to know lots of girls and boys. I have never seen the Peters' home, but I'm sure it is lovely. They are quite well off—your father was a doctor, or would have been—you could do the same. I'm always here, and your room will be there for you. On the other hand you could stay here. I don't know what you'd do when you finish school, but I'm sure we would manage—we always have done. Sleep on it and we'll talk again."

Cassie had made her decision. She and Molly would go to England, they would see the school and enjoy the trip.

Molly wrote to Edward Peters to tell him. They arranged dates, and one day Molly got a large envelope in the post with first class tickets from Enniskillen to Haslemere in Surrey. Molly had always saved the money Edward had sent to Cassie for birthdays and Christmas—now she took out enough to buy Cassie the sort of clothes she thought she would be expected to have. She also spent a lot of the money Joe had been paying her for clothes for herself.

The day before they were due to leave, Cassie invited Sam to tea. He knew how much he would miss her, and didn't want to think how empty his life would be without her. He took some money out of his savings and went to Enniskillen—he wanted to give her a present. He looked all round the shops and couldn't see anything—then passing an old antique shop he saw what he wanted. It was a brooch like a bunch of violets—the leaves were green enamel and the flowers little mauve stones. It cost him one pound, but the old man in the shop said the stones were amethysts and that it was mounted on silver. He polished it and put it into a little green velvet box.

Sam kept looking at it—it twinkled back when the light caught it. When the meal was over and he handed the little box to Cassie, she opened it and gasped.

"Sam, it is beautiful—where did you find it? Oh look Mammie, isn't it just beautiful!."

"This must have cost you a lot of money Sam," Molly said.

"It's not really new—I found it in an antique shop, a very old dusty shop," Sam said.

Molly said, "It will look lovely on the lapel of your new green costume."

"That's what I'm wearing tomorrow—oh thank you, Sam." Cassie was bubbling with excitement.

They sat down at the piano and played a duet together, then Molly played some old songs and sang—her lovely clear soprano ringing out. Joe and Kathleen could hear her in their house—Joe hummed along, but Kathleen was restless and kept looking at the clock, going in and out to the kitchen. At 9 o'clock she went upstairs and stood at her bedroom window. Sam and Cassie stood at the gate. She watched as Cassie put her arms around Sam's neck and kissed him. He held her and kissed her in return. They stood there holding each other for a couple of minutes, then they kissed again.

Eventually Cassie went indoors, and Sam watched her go before coming home. Kathleen hurried down the stairs as he came through the back door—he was crying, and walked on up the stairs to his bedroom. Kathleen shook with rage—how dare that child make her son cry.

She stoked up the fire and put the kettle on as Joe came into the kitchen. "Are you making tea," he asked.

"Yes," she replied sharply.

Joe wondered what had upset her. "Is Sam in?"

"Yes," she repeated.

At this he locked the door, and sat down to drink his tea. Kathleen didn't speak, so Joe got up and said goodnight and went to his room. He was just dozing when he heard voices, and got up. Sam's room, he thought—what is going on?, He went in and Kathleen was on her knees beside Sam's bed, sobbing. I don't want you kissing Cassie, she's no good like her mother. You must kiss only me, please Sam, hold me and kiss me.

Sam saw his father across Kathleen's head. "Take her away, please Dad," he begged, "she is making me sick."

Kathleen jumped to her feet, "That's right," she said, "run to your father—he is as bad as you—both your heads are turned by these two next door. They are both whores, both of them—I am glad they are going away and I hope they never come back."

Joe counted to ten. He wanted to beat Kathleen to silence her—he didn't know she knew such language. Eventually he said gently,

"Come away Kathleen, you don't know what you are saying—come to your bed."

He held her arm as he led her to her room. She was sobbing like a child. He put his arm around her and wiped her tears. "Get into bed, it will be better in the morning," he said, tucking her in—then left her and went back to Sam who was still sobbing.

"What was all that about?" Joe asked.

"Cassie kissed me goodbye at the gate—I bought her a little present and she kissed me for it. We've often kissed—she is like a sister, and so is Molly. Mother must have been watching from her bedroom. Is she going mad?"

"No," said Joe, "she's jealous of Molly and Cassie. I spend all day working with Molly and you spend all your spare time with Cassie. We will have to be nicer to your mother, Sam. I think we have been neglecting her."

"I'll never forgive her for speaking like that about Cassie and Molly. I was fed up with her always cuddling and kissing me when we lived at Archdale. It was great having my own room at last. I was ashamed in case the boys at school found out where I was sleeping. I love this house, if only Mother would leave me alone."

Joe didn't know what to say. He knew everything Sam said was true, so he changed tactics and said, "You will be leaving school soon—what do you want to do?"

"I always meant to go and work with Grandad Scarlett, but now he's dead and the workshop is gone, I'll have to look around."

"Now Molly's away I will need a bit of help in the garden," Joe said. "Just until Molly gets back—in the meantime you can look around. I'd love you to carry on with the market garden, but I want you to be happy, Sam. I really love you, and I'm glad you kissed Cassie—she is a lovely child. I may go down and kiss her goodbye myself in the morning. We are both going to miss them."

• • •

Kathleen looked haggard and pale next morning. Joe tried to talk to her about what needed doing in the garden, but Sam ignored her when she spoke to him.

The school had closed for the holidays, and Sam and Joe went to work. Kathleen cleaned the house, made the beds, and prepared dinners—all the time she was waiting for Molly and Cassie to come round and say goodbye. She didn't know how to face them, and when Joe and Sam came in for elevens, she said she had a headache and was going to lie down.

At twelve thirty she heard the hired car arrive. Sam helped Molly to carry out the luggage. Kathleen watched, standing well away from the window. Molly wore a smart brown costume and a cream straw hat with a wide brown ribbon; Cassie had on a sage green costume and a matching straw boater—both had their hair in a coil at the back. Kathleen hated them, they looked so smart. Sam was laughing and Joe came and shook hands with Molly, then kissed Cassie's cheek and wished her will. "Hurry back," he called to Molly as they drove away. Kathleen lay down on her bed and wept.

The next few days felt empty and dull for Joe. He and Sam worked hard, and Kathleen started spring cleaning. She washed paint work, curtains, blankets and bed spreads, she bought paint and painted the staircase, she beat carpets and mats and polished lino and furniture. On Friday she cooked and baked, and her stall looked like a banquet. She sold out and walked wearily indoors. Joe and Sam tidied away the stalls and came in.

The kettle was boiling, and Kathleen started to get up and make the tea—but Joe said, "Sit where you are, Kathleen. I'll do it, you look all in." He called to Sam, "Bring in the bread and cheese and whatever else you want—your mother is tired."

Sam laid the table, and they sat down to eat. Joe poured out a second cup of tea and said, "Tomorrow let's all go for a picnic. I've never been to the top of Monument Hill—let's go up there. There's a bus going to Enniskillen at twelve o'clock, we could go on that."

"How will we get back?" Kathleen asked.

"We will hire a car," Joe said.

"I was going to cook a chicken for dinner tomorrow," she said.

"Cook it later today—we can take it with us, with bread and butter and a bit of salad."

"There's an apple tart as well."

"There you are then," Joe said. "Now we only need the sun to shine."

The weather was kind, the sun shone all day, and the steep climb up Monument Hill left them breathless. They found a bench and sat to catch their breath. Kathleen shared out the food. There was a nice breeze, but very few people about. A scruffy little black and white dog came sniffing around—Sam threw a piece of bread, which it grabbed and ate quickly.

"It seems to be hungry," Sam said, throwing another piece.

"Don't encourage it," Kathleen said, "dogs are awful scroungers."

"I'd scrounge if I was hungry," Sam replied. "I'd love a dog."

"We don't want dogs or cats in the house," Kathleen said, "they bring dirt and fleas."

Joe looked at her in despair. She had a chance to do something Sam would like, and she had spoiled it. Sam didn't say anything. He found a small stick and threw it—the little dog ran and fetched and brought it to him, and he played like this all the afternoon.

At six thirty, Joe found a hired car and they came home. It had been a great day—Kathleen talked to both of them and, although Sam didn't say much to his mother, they didn't argue.

Joe had been seriously thinking about getting a dog, but he wanted it to be part of the family. Kathleen's attitude made that impossible, so he let it rest. He had a notion that Molly would like a dog now that Cassie had gone—he would get one for her when she came back if she wanted one. Sam could share it with her—no doubt Kathleen would have something to say about it, but Joe had decided that the world didn't revolve around Kathleen's likes and dislikes. She would have to like it or lump it. If Molly wanted a dog she would have one.

• • •

Molly and Cassie sat in the first class carriage on the train to Belfast. Molly grinned. "I feel frightful posh," she said.

"Don't be common Mama." Cassie put on a plumy voice, and they both giggled.

"I'm going to enjoy this," Molly said. "The only thing is, do you think we will ever get there? That list from your Grandfather sounds complicated, and I'm just a poor ignorant little country bumpkin. I can hardly read his writing."

Cassie fell about laughing. "Mam, please try to be serious, at least when we get there. They may not have a sense of humour—we could look like a couple of idiots."

"I thought that's what we are," Molly replied.

In Belfast they went to the docks, and as their boat wasn't sailing until eleven that evening they went and had a meal before going aboard. The stewardess showed them to their two-berth cabin, which was small but comfortable.

At six o'clock in the morning she brought them tea and thin bread and butter. "We dock at seven," she said, "and you can have breakfast in the dining room, but they also do a good breakfast in the restaurant at Heysham—your choice." They thanked her and decided to eat in the restaurant, as their train wouldn't leave till ten o'clock. It took four and a half hours to reach Euston, and then they would have to get to Waterloo—but first that breakfast.

They ordered bacon and eggs with toast and tea, and sat over it until nine o'clock—then, after walking for a while, they got on the train to Euston. It stopped at Crewe for thirty minutes and Cassie bought newspapers and chocolate, then at last they arrived at Euston. It was large and dirty, and they quickly found a cab to Waterloo—driving through London was a great experience for them both—and one and a half hours later the train pulled into Haslemere Station.

A tall grey-haired man walked smartly towards them. "That's him," Molly whispered.

"Hello, at last." Edward Peters came towards them, both hands held out, and put an arm around each of them and kissed their cheeks.

A porter hovered in the background. "Just the two cases, eh Molly? Right Stan, take them to the car."

The porter walked in front of them, and Edward, with one on each side, was smiling like a Cheshire cat.

"This is the biggest moment—I have waited for years to see you two," he said as he hugged them again.

Stan put the cases the car boot, and Edward tossed him a coin. "Thanks guv," he grinned.

"How are your family Stan?" Edward asked.

"All fine sir. "I've got ten grandchildren now."

Edward touched his shoulder. "Good for you," he said gently.

"You know him well?" Molly asked as they drove away.

"Yes, I used to go to London every day by train. Stan was always there, cheerful and happy. The locals jokingly say that his mother had him on the platform and left him here, and that he's been here ever since. But he fought in the war and was wounded several times and afterwards he couldn't work—then this job of porter came up and he took it. He has six children—they are all grown up now—and though he's had a hard life, I've never seen him unhappy.

Molly sat in the passenger seat and Cassie in the back.

"It's only ten minutes now. I expect you are both tired—Helen will have tea ready."

Molly smiled. "I can't think of anything nicer," she said.

They climbed the hill into Hindhead and over the cross roads.

"That road we have just crossed is the Portsmouth to London road," he told them. A minute later they turned into a driveway and stopped in front of a big grey house.

Two golden Labradors came running up, tails wagging furiously, and greeted Edward, then Cassie. She patted their heads, and stroked them. "Are they yours?" she asked.

"Yes," her grandfather said, "this one is Whiskey and that one is Brandy." Cassie and Molly laughed at this. "Well," Edward said, "I had to call them something, and that was the first thing that came into my head."

A small, slim lady came out of the door—she looked frail, but walked well—hugged Cassie and kissed Molly. Then she looked into Cassie's face..

"You have your father's eyes," she said softly, "and your mother's wonderful hair. Welcome to England—we have waited a long time for this day. Come in, tea is ready."

They followed Helen down the long hall and to the left. The tea table was laid in a lovely conservatory, surrounded by plants, and five or six basket chairs with gay floral cushions were set out around the low table. A middle-aged maid carried in the teapot and hot water.

"This is Anne," Helen said. "She came with us from Dublin, and Lizzy is the cook. They are both Irish. You will meet Lizzy later."

Anne smiled at them and said, "Welcome to Surrey."

Helen poured the tea, and there were little cucumber sandwiches, scones with cream and strawberry jam, and a big fruit cake. They talked about the garden and the journey.

"You are very quiet, Cassie," Helen said.

Molly answered for her, "This has all been a big adventure for her,. By tomorrow she will have found her tongue, she is anything but quiet." Cassie blushed.

After tea Helen showed them their rooms. Anne had taken their cases up, and Helen said, "You will have to decide which rooms you want—they are together and the bathroom is opposite. Have a bath if you want to, there is plenty of hot water, and have a lie down when you're unpacked. Dinner is at seven thirty."

"Do we have to dress up?" Molly asked.

"Not really," Helen said, "I usually just change my dress. Wear whatever is comfortable—it's so good to have you here."

Left on their own they explored the two bedrooms, both large and well furnished, the windows open to the afternoon sun. The bathroom was a great novelty. They usually bathed in a tin bath in front of the kitchen fire—this was real luxury. Thick soft towels, beautifully scented soap.

Anne knocked and offered to help them unpack. Cassie wanted to talk to her, so she let her help and they chatted while they worked.

"Mrs Peters has been so much better since she heard you were coming," Anne said. "She never really got over Mister Teddy's death. She nearly died at the time—she couldn't keep any food down and she got thinner and thinner. She had to go into hospital for a time—she still eats very little and is often poorly in winter—but now you are here, she will pick up. You are very beautiful, Miss Cassie—I hope your stay and be happy."

After dinner they went into the drawing room. It was very big, and there were double French windows leading out to three semicircular steps which led into the garden. There were also fat cosy chairs and sofas, and at the far end near a corner window was a grand piano.

Anne put the coffee tray down and Edward poured for them. There was a glass of milk for Cassie, and after she had drunk it she wandered over to the piano.

"This is lovely," she said, and lifted the lid.

"Do you play?" Edward asked.

"A little," she said, "but I've never played a Grand before."

"There's sheet music in the stool," said Helen.

Cassie went through the sheets, and found a slightly dog-eared one which she chose and started to play. Molly wondered if she had done the wrong thing. Edward stood looking out of the window, and Helen sat with her eyes closed but tears running down her cheeks. Cassie played on, sometimes softly, then louder and finally ending with three soft notes.

Edward blew his nose and wiped his eyes. He came over and put his arms around her.

"That, my dear, was beautiful. It was Teddy's favourite, and we haven't heard it since we lost him."

Molly took Helen's soft white hand in hers. "I'm sorry mother," she said, "I didn't even know that Teddy played the piano—we have upset you, I'm sorry."

Helen smiled, and held on to Molly's hand. "I'm not upset, it just brought back memories—Cassie plays so well."

Cassie picked up a music book, turned the pages and started playing again. This time everyone smiled—it was the Belfast Horn Pipe, and soon her three listeners were tapping their feet, and all applauded when she finished.

"Now I think it is time you went to bed," Molly said. "It's nine thirty."

After Cassie had kissed them good night and gone to bed, Molly came up an hour later and found her fast asleep. She kissed her forehead. "I'm proud of you darling," she whispered.

The next morning, Molly woke up and wondered where she was—then she remembered—in England with Teddy's parent. How had all this come about? She looked at the clock—six a.m.—got out of bed and opened the curtains. It was a lovely morning and the birds were singing. Opening the door softly, she looked into Cassie's room and a bright head popped out.

"Hello Mam, I've been lying here wondering what on earth I'm doing here."

Molly smiled, "So have I. Do you feel like a walk? It's a glorious morning."

They dressed and tiptoed downstairs and through to the back. In the back porch, the Labradors lay in their baskets.

"Hello boys," whispered Cassie, "feel like a walk?" She reached up and took their leads off the hook.

Leading a dog each, they walked down to the bottom of the garden. There was a small gate which they went through, past some big trees, and there in front of them lay a huge bowl. The heather was blooming and they stood and stared.

"Let's walk down—there's a path. The dogs will know—they've been here before, I think," said Cassie. They walked down and down—it seemed never ending. Then they stood and looked up. It was as though they had been swallowed.

"I wonder what it's called," Molly said. "I'll bet Teddy used to walk down here when he was a boy."

They climbed back up and sat on the heather at the top. Then finally they made their way back. The dogs were thirsty—Molly picked their bowl up and went into the kitchen to fill it. Two startled pairs of eyes met her as she walked in.

"Good morning Anne!," Molly said, " and this must be Lizzy."

She held out her had and Lizzy took it. "Pleased to meet you Miss Molly," she said.

Cassie, hearing the voices, came in. "And this is Miss Cassie," said Molly.

Lizzy held out her arms and Cassie came and kissed her. "It is so good to see you both at last—you will put a heartbeat back in this house."

"I was just going to take up your early morning tea," Annie said.

"Let's drink it here," said Cassie. "We have just had the most marvellous walk into a great bowl full of heather."

"Ah," said Lizzy, "that's The Devil's Punch Bowl."

"What a wonderful name," Molly said, "how did it get like that do you know?"

"Ask Master," Lizzy said, "he's the one for to ask—he will tell you all about it."

Molly and Cassie left the kitchen, their lovely hair streaming down their backs.

"There's a couple of beauties right enough," Lizzy said, "and so friendly."

• • •

The breakfast gong sounded. Molly and Cassie had made their beds and tidied their rooms and washed. Molly said, "Do you think I could have my hair down? It makes my head ache when it's piled up."

"Why not?" Cassie answered. Tie it with a bow at the back."

"What about shoes? Do you think I could go barefooted?"

"No Mother, put you shoes on like a good girl."

Molly laughed. "Maybe they will make a lady out of you, but I don't think I'd qualify."

Cassie hugged her. "You are the most beautiful lady I know" she said.

They had breakfast with Edward—he said Helen had hers in bed. Molly was asking him about the Punch Bowl when Cassie asked to be excused and ran up stairs. She paused by the first door on the landing, then knocked softly and went in.

Helen was sitting up with her breakfast tray on her lap. "Why it's Cassie, good morning darling, did you sleep well?"

"Very well, thank you Grandmother. How are you this morning?"

"Wonderfully well." Helen smiled. "Lizzy usually sends up tea and toast, but I seem to have a boiled egg this morning."

"Well she will be awfully disappointed if you don't eat it—it's a lovely brown egg, I've just had one too. This is a lovely place, Grandmother. Mam and I went for a walk with the dogs at six o'clock this morning—we went down into the Devil's Punch Bowl. Grandad is telling Mamma all about it in the dining room. I thought I'd like to keep you company, and make you eat your egg."

"Do you always get up at six o'clock in the morning?" Helen asked.

"I don't usually, but Mamma gets up at five thirty most mornings. She works in the market garden next door—it's owned by Mr and Mrs Lyons who live in the cottage next to ours. Their son Sam is my best friend—we go to school together, and take piano lessons together on Saturday mornings. My Uncle Fred and his family own the farm— they own the ground where the market garden is, but they lease it to Joe Lyons."

"So you buy your vegetables from Mr Lyons," Helen said.

"Oh no, we never buy vegetables. Mammie has a great vegetable garden—we have plums, apples and raspberries as well, and lots of flowers."

"It sounds very nice," said Helen.

"It's lovely—I love the cottage and the school and our little church. Mammie and I are very happy. I'm glad to meet you and Grandad, and I love this house, but I'll always belong to Fermanagh— it's lovely too. You know we are quite near Lough Erne—it's three hundred and sixty five miles round and there are fifty two islands— isn't that strange? The old people say there were seven monasteries on the islands. If there were, there are only ruins now. The most famous island is Devonish—there's lots of ruins and an old cemetery there. We took a boat out to it from the school—it was really creepy.

• • •

Molly had been away for a week. Joe missed her, but Sam worked well. Two postcards had arrived, one for Sam from Cassie with a picture of Hindhead, and the other addressed to Mr and Mrs Lyons was a picture of the Devil's Punch Bowl. They both said they were enjoying their holiday, and that it was warmer in the South of England than in the North of Ireland. Molly said, 'see you all soon.' Sam put his card on the wall in his bedroom.

He and Joe were sitting down for a rest when Sam said, "Dad, do you think I could have a bicycle?"

"You know, Sam, I was just thinking that myself the other day. We will go into town Saturday afternoon and you can pick one."

Sitting at their evening meal, Sam said to Kathleen, "Dad is buying me a bike on Saturday."

Joe waited for Kathleen to object, but she said, "I've been thinking, I'd like a bicycle myself."

"Could you ride a bike?" Sam asked.

"Yes," said Kathleen. "I learned to ride Auntie Anna's bicycle before she got married. She's had a bike for ages.

Joe laughed. "I'd better polish my old daisy-cutter up—it hasn't been out of the shed for ages."

"Get a new one Dad," Sam said.

"No," replied his father, "that one will do nicely for now."

Sam got his bicycle—the one he wanted—and Joe was happy to pay for it. He had been a model son since Cassie left. Kathleen hadn't mentioned her or Molly again, but she didn't talk much at all. The house was as clean as ever, the washing and ironing done and the meals were always ready, but Joe felt that she was an explosion waiting to go off. He wanted her to buy a new bicycle, but she said a second hand one would do for her.

Sam asked Joe if he could have the afternoon off one day, and Joe agreed. He wondered where he was going, but didn't ask. He knew Kathleen would ask, and she did.

"I'm just going out on my bike," Sam answered her, "I'll be back in time for tea."

He rode his bike to Enniskillen. He remembered looking down an alley and seeing a lot of timber piled up, and walked along until he found the place. The gate to the alley was open and he went in. There were great piles of timber and a large shed, and he could hear the saws going and a lot of hammering inside. He looked in and a young man came up to him.

"Can I help you?" he asked.

"I was looking for the owner," Sam said.

"I'm the owner's son," the man replied. "My father is out, but he'll be back soon. I've just made tea—would you like a mug?"

"I would," Sam said. "I've just ridden in from Lisbellaw, and it's a warm day."

They sat with their tea, and Sam said, "I'm looking for a job—I wondered if you needed any one."

"Why do you want to work here?"

"I'd always planned to work with my Grandad. He was a cabinet maker and had his own business, but he died last year and the place closed down. My Uncle Robert learned the trade with him, but opened his own shop in Portadown—he is doing very well, but he has two sons of his own and it's too far away in any case. I could stay and work with my father—he has a market garden—but I always said I'd work with wood."

Just then an older man came in. He poured himself a mug of tea, looked at Sam and said, "You're Joe Lyons' boy aren't you? I see you working away every Saturday morning when I take my wife for her vegetables."

"Sam wants to work here," the son said. "His grandfather was a cabinet maker, but he's died.

"Would that be John Scarlett?" the man asked.

"Yes," said Sam, "did you know him?"

"He used to buy wood from me," the man replied, "he was a great man, and a craftsman. He made the famous Scarlett Roses—you'll find his furniture in all the best houses around here."

"What do you make here?" Sam asked.

"Mostly doors and window frames, sheds and just lately we've been making greenhouses. So you want a job? I'll give you a trial, Sam—ten shillings per week, five and a half days, start at eight o'clock one week from Monday."

"Right," said Sam, "I'll be here, thank you."

Sam arrived home as Kathleen dished up the tea.

"Did you enjoy your ride?" Joe asked.

"I did," said Sam, "and I'm starting work at Preston's timber yard a week Monday."

"You could have consulted us first," Kathleen said. "Your father needs help in the garden."

"Molly will be back—I'll be here until then," Sam said. "They make doors and window frames and sheds, and they go out to the houses, and fit them—I think I'll like it there. Mr Preston knew Grandad Scarlett, and his wife buys her vegetables here on Saturdays."

"Oh yes," said Joe, "I know her—she spends a lot of money here, and she buys her eggs and butter off the farm stall. I expect she buys cakes from you, Kathleen."

"I don't know," Kathleen said, "they all look the same to me. I hope they are going to pay you, Sam."

"Of course they are," Sam said, but he didn't say how much.

• • •

When Molly came back, Joe looked up and saw her lugging her suitcase along from the bus stop. He ran down the field and took it from her. "Why didn't you take a taxi from the station?" he asked.

"Because the holiday is over," she said. "I've spent a lot money and Cassie is settled. I'm going in to take my shoes off, and I won't put them on again until I go to church on Sunday. How are you all, and how is Sam? I've got a letter for him from Cassie."

Joe put the case down in the kitchen and took her in his arms. "Welcome home, my darling." He kissed her again and again.

"Joe stop it, Kathleen is next door—I'm sure she watched me coming in, and you carrying my case. Go back to work—I'll come round later."

He went back up the field and started working, but he felt like skipping along the furrow.

Sam had started his new job two days ago. The five mile ride morning and evening didn't bother him, and he was full of chatter about his day and what he had done. Joe listened and asked questions, but Kathleen said very little. She cut Sam's sandwiches and put in a piece of cake and an apple, then called him and gave him his breakfast. When he finished he just picked up his dinner bag, said cheerio, and left.

Kathleen did her baking and house work, and then asked Joe what he wanted her to do in the greenhouses. Each day was the same. She seemed to have lost Sam—he never made physical contact with her, and if she was near him he edged away. When he went into his bed-room he always closed the door—she felt completely shut out.

One day when she went to the little shop and post office, she saw a card in the window: 'Ladies Bicycle for sale, nearly new, two pounds.' She got the address from the shop keeper, and found it was quite near. When she asked the lady why she was selling it, the young woman smiled.

"I'm expecting a baby in three months time. I won't be riding the bicycle and I need the money to help buy a pram."

So Kathleen got her bicycle, and decided to ride into Enniskillen. She wanted to see where Sam worked, but she didn't tell Joe—he would have been furious with her. She found the place and wheeled the bike up and down looking into the yard, but she didn't go in, and she didn't see Sam. Mr Preston, sitting in his office, saw her and wondered what she wanted, but he decided to stay where he was. 'If she wants Sam she can come and ask to see him,' he thought.

● ● ●

Molly had come around the evening she got back, bringing them all a present. She gave Kathleen a small soft packet, containing a pair of cream gloves, very soft, and trimmed with tan and three creamy pearl buttons at the wrist.

"Thank you very much, Molly—I've been trying to find cream gloves for ages."

"I think the size is right," Molly said. "Your hands are about the same size as mine."

There was a very useful penknife for Sam, with four blades, a corkscrew and bottle opener. He was delighted—he had wanted one for ages.

"Mind you don't cut yourself," Kathleen said.

Joe and Molly's eyes met for a second, and Molly hastily handed him his present. It was a tie pin with a Shetland pony's head on a straight gold bar.

"Ah, this brings back memories," he said. "It's lovely."

"Do you remember the Shetlands, Sam?" said Molly. "I wonder how they are all doing? We could go on our bikes one Sunday to see them."

"Oh Sam is a working man now, Molly," Joe said.

Sam blushed. "Well, I am since Monday morning." He told her about Mr Preston and how he had remembered his grandfather.

"I think everyone knew your grandfather Sam—he was a wonderful craftsman," Molly said.

"The Orange March is in Newtownbutler on the twelfth," Joe said. "We're all meeting there, all Kathleen's family. Robert and Eileen and the boys are going to stay with Grandma Scarlett, it will be nice for her. Anna and George live quite near there, so they will be going on their bikes, and I believe Thomas and Eleanor are going to hire a car. Of course John and Harold are in the band and Thomas will be marching with Wattlebridge Lodge—he's a great Orange man is Thomas."

"Will you be coming to the March, Molly," Kathleen asked.

"I don't think so," Molly said. "I love the massed bands, but I think it is very hard on the Catholic community."

"I'm surprised to hear you say that," Kathleen said. "I always thought of you as a staunch Protestant."

"I'm a Protestant, yes," said Molly. "When I was a midwife in Dublin I delivered Protestant and Catholic babies—I often knelt on the bare floor where a poor Catholic mother lay with sometimes a dozen children already. A lot of the babies didn't survive, and a few mothers died too."

"But surely there were poor Protestant families too," said Kathleen.

"I'm sure there were," Molly answered, "but I never delivered a Protestant baby on the floor—they all had beds."

"The last time I attended a Twelfth of July March," Molly went on, "I listened to Sir Basil Brooke shouting from the speaker's platform, that he didn't and wouldn't employ a Catholic on his estate. I wanted to go up and challenge him, but my brother held me back." She smiled then. "You all go to the march I'll look after the greenhouses that day."

"I didn't know Molly had political views," said Kathleen after Molly had gone home. "She seems to side with the Catholics."

Sam looked up. "I think Molly would help anyone. She is right to think that every man who wants to work should have a job, and I for one agree with her."

"I hope you don't start airing your views to the family on the twelfth," Kathleen said.

"Well now, that depends. I will stick to my views whoever is listening, but I won't start the argument."

"Peter Monk was a Catholic, and his family," Joe said. "I've never met a more honest man nor a better worker, and I'm sure there are a lot of lazy Protestants about."

"Uncle Johnny for instance," said Sam.

"I won't have you speak like that about my brother," Kathleen said.

"But, Mother," Sam answered, "you've come back yourself and told us that he does nothing on the farm, and that he has sold off the cattle—I'd say he is lazy."

• • •

Eileen Scarlett sat at her desk in the little glass enclosure in the corner of the shop. She tidied the papers, putting each in the right folder, everything in order. The finished furniture had been delivered and had been paid for—that was usually the worrying part, getting the money in after the deliveries—but the cheques were in the bank, the new orders well under way, and she and Robert were having a rare week-end off. Robert's mother, Jane Scarlett, was having a get-together—all the families were coming and Eileen would be able to go and see her parents as well, but she enjoyed visiting the Scarlett family.

Robert had worked hard when they first came here after the war. He had bought a motor van for deliveries, having just learned to drive—then two years ago they found themselves nearly squeezed out of the flat over the shop, as they had no more space in the work shop.

So he had bought a house in the suburbs, three bedrooms and set in a nice garden.

He suggested getting an office girl so that Eileen could stay at home and look after the house, but she hated housework and said she knew the office work like the back of her hand. She put a notice in the shop window for a housekeeper, and found a cheerful person in her middle forties, a widow named Jean McClusky with two grown-up children. She came in at ten o'clock, tidied and cleaned the house, did the washing and ironing and left a meal ready on the stove before she finished at 4.30. She was paid well over the going rate, but she was worth it, and cheaper than an office girl. And the house was always spick and span.

Eileen smiled to herself when she remembered Kathleen teaching her to darn socks. Nowadays, she looked at all the socks and the one's with holes she threw in the bin, but she believed Jean McClusky took them home and washed and darned them. She didn't mind—she had bought a hundred pairs at a sale, and there were still plenty left.

Robert had now bought a car, and they were travelling the forty miles into Fermanagh this evening. Monday coming was the twelfth July, and they were all going to have a good time.

She had made up the pay packets for the men—eight now including her son John: five on woodwork, two upholsterers and a French polisher. Business had eased off a little, but was a bit more up-market. Genuine gentry were buying and having old furniture replaced— the old Victorian heavy, clumsy stuff was being replaced by light and more elegant styles.

The eldest son John was a quiet young man. He worked well and did as he was told, but Robert wondered how interested he really was. He had no ambition—just earned his money. Edmund, who liked to be called Ed, was different. He asked if he could attend a new College in Belfast. In the woodwork department, he studied books on French and Italian furniture and Robert was delighted with him. He wanted to travel on the continent and look at some of the old homes and the workshops restoring old furniture, and Robert was prepared to let him go.

Eileen looked very smart. Her figure had always been good. She wore dark suits with snowy blouses, her faintly polished nails and slim white hands adorned by a couple of nice rings which Robert had bought her. He was very proud of her—they had had a bad beginning, and then the war and Robert away for three and half years. They had weathered the storm and were a good team.

The twelfth July was a beautiful day—the Orangemen were usually lucky with the weather. There were thirty lodges and their bands from all over Co. Fermanagh.

Robert and Eileen pleaded with Jane to come with them in their car. "Mother, all the family will be together—we will take food and flasks and all have a good talk."

At last she agreed to come—she was looking forward to seeing Kathleen, Joe and Sam, and Anna and George. Anna didn't get to see her as often as Eleanor and Kathleen did.

They watched the bands and lodges march past from a low wall near the pavement and had a good view. John and Harold McMahon, playing flutes in Wattlebridge band, waved to them as they went by. The field they were all heading for was large and flat, with a raised platform in the middle for the speakers. Around the sides were stalls selling fruit, sweets, lemonade and souvenirs.

Eileen and Robert spread two large rugs.

"Can we move away from the speakers platform so we can talk among ourselves?" Jane said.

Sam laughed. "You don't want to hear what they have to say."

"Sam dear, I've been listening to it since I was half your age—they hardly ever change the tune."

Everyone laughed at that except Thomas. He was wearing his orange sash with metallic braid and wanted to listen. He was surprised at his mother-in-law at first, but then realised that she had her entire family around her, and of course she wanted to talk to them. So he lingered while the families moved away.

Seated on the rugs, the women handed round the sandwiches and tea. Everyone had brought food, and there was plenty. Robert's son, Ed, was looking at Polly. He hadn't seen her for years, and eventually got up saying, "Come on cousin Polly, lets walk round the stalls, I'll buy you a present," and they walked off holding hands.

Jessica watched them go. She wished someone would take her round the stalls. Polly looked very nice today, she thought. Mother had made them both new dresses—Polly's was pale yellow and Mother had done her hair up this morning with bits of rag in ringlets tied at the back with yellow ribbon; Jessica's dress was white with red polka dots and Eleanor had plaited her long dark hair and tied a red ribbon on it.

"Try not to lose that ribbon," she had said.

Jessica reached round and pulled her plait—the ribbon was gone. She looked around and saw it lying on the grass, picked it up, undid the bow and started to roll up the ribbon. Her Uncle Robert lay in front of her, flat on his back. He had taken off his jacket and folded it under his head. The grown-ups were all talking—Jessica was bored. She reached over and drew the ribbon across Uncle Robert's nose. He smiled, but didn't open his eyes. She did it again and he grabbed her wrist, turned over on his stomach and smiled at her. He's just like Grandad, she thought, Grandad without a beard.

"Are you bored?" he whispered. She nodded. "So am I, let's take a walk." He took her hand and they moved away.

Jane and her daughter-in-law Eileen were sitting together.

"I wish I had a daughter," Eileen said.

Eleanor heard. "I'll let you have that one," she laughed, indicating the departing Jessica. She's one person's work."

"Your father loved her," Jane said. "She's always very good when she stays with me."

"I think she'd be better if Pat Cassidy wasn't there—together they are lethal."

• • •

Robert and Jessica walked along the stalls, and stopped at one with jewellery on.

"Which one, Jessie?" he asked.

"A necklace for me?"

"Yes, your choice."

Jessica studied them and picked up a bright red one, large delph beads in front grading to smaller ones at the back. Robert put it round her neck.

"Yes," he said, "that's the one."

He paid for it—a shilling. Jessica was stunned—she now owned a necklace which cost a shilling. Then they moved on to the fruit stall, where he bought a punnet of strawberries.

"We'll sit here and eat them all," he said.

Jessica had thought they were to share with everyone. Sitting close together, Robert found the biggest strawberry and handed it to her. She ate it—delicious—and soon the punnet was empty.

"Now you won't be sick and disgrace us?" he asked.

"No fear," said Jessica, "I can eat anything."

When they got back, Jessica showed off her necklace. Bill the baby tried to pull it, and she slapped his hand away. He cried, so Joe Lyons picked him up and cuddled him.

"I can see by your fingers and around your mouth that Uncle Robert bought more than the necklace," said Eleanor.

The bands were beginning to assembly again—they were going to march back through the town. Jane was tired and Robert helped her to the car.

"Can Jessica come with me?" she asked.

"Of course," said Robert, "there's plenty of room." He got the car out before the parade, and stopped near the end of the town. "We can sit in here in comfort and watch the end."

They watched until the last one, a silver band, in red and navy uniform, stood close to the car and played the lovely hymn 'The day Thou giveth, Lord is ended'. Jessica thought it was beautiful. She looked at her grandmother, and tears were streaming down her cheeks. Jessica hugged her.

"What's wrong, Gran?"

"That was Grandad's favourite," she said, "wouldn't you think they knew."

Robert's son John disgraced himself by disappearing, and no-one could find him when it was time to leave. John and Harold McMahon had marched with their band, and they said John had been with some old school friends.

"Mother is tired and wants to get home," said Robert. "John will have to find his own way—I hope he turns up by morning, as we're leaving early."

John turned up just after midnight. He had been drinking and had been sick, and was in a disgusting state. The back door had been left open for him, and Robert heard him come in. He cleaned him up and waited until next day when they got back to Portadown to talk to him.

When he asked where he had started drinking, to Robert's and Eileen's astonishment John said he had been having a drink at weekends for about four years. He said he didn't usually get drunk, but had met a few old friends and things had got out of hand. Robert told him it was a bad habit and an awful waste of money. John, placid as ever, agreed with him, but his weekend drinking continued.

Jessica was very proud of her necklace. Ed had bought one for Polly, who boasted that her pale blue necklace had cost nine pence and Ed had also bought a banana for her. Jessica said proudly, "Mine cost one shilling and we ate a whole punnet of strawberries between us." Uncle Robert was her hero, and he looked just like Grandad.

• • •

Kathleen had enjoyed the twelfth. The family gathering had been warm and friendly, and Anna and George seemed happy, although

Anna, who had always looked young was beginning to show her age. Her soft skin was sun-tanned and a few wrinkles had appeared round her eyes. She had never worked in the fields until her marriage, but she looked well, and was nicely dressed. Eleanor, for all that she had six children, still looked young and was full of life. Kathleen thought they were a lovely family. She could see Eleanor and Thomas had made a great effort to dress them all, the boys in suits and white shirts and the girls in pretty dresses.

Sam had had the time of his life with all his cousins. Kathleen wished wistfully that he would laugh more at home. He never joked with her, nor told her anything. She deeply regretted the scene she made the night before Cassie went away, and she had hoped he would forget it—but Sam was frightened to get too close to her. He didn't want her running his life.

Joe had enjoyed the day too. It was good to talk to Thomas and Robert, and see how much Sam enjoyed being with the family. He wondered where John Scarlett had got to, and thought maybe he had met some girl—but the lad was twenty, a grown man.

When he had cuddled Eleanor's baby, he had thought of Molly— all alone in his garden, her family at the parade, her daughter gone away. She must be feeling lonely, he longed for her warm presence, her happy laugh—he must see her alone soon.

That evening Kathleen had wanted to go back to her Mother's, but for once Joe was adamant. He must get home. It had been a hot day and all his gardens needed watering. He couldn't expect Molly to do it all.

"You go back with the family, Kathleen. Sam and I can manage. Stay a couple of days if you want to."

Urged by her family she agreed. He and Sam found Molly busy in the greenhouse. The tomatoes needed water—with all the windows and doors open it was still over eighty degrees. Joe sprayed the hose pipe on the roof and cooled it down.

"I was afraid they were dying," said Molly, inviting Sam and Joe in for tea. "It's only salad, but it's been so hot I didn't cook."

Sam said he had been eating all day, but he enjoyed his salad, and afterwards announced that he was going down to the Orange Hall where there was a dance. All his friends were going.

"Enjoy yourself," Joe said.

"I may be back late—do you mind?"

"I'll leave the back door open. Just don't drink, please Sam, and come in quietly. I need my sleep."

106

Joe and Molly waited until Sam had gone, then they were in each others arms.

"It's been a long, lonely day," Molly whispered.

"I guessed that," Joe replied. "I was thinking what a selfish person I am leaving you here alone."

They went upstairs and lay in each others arms, slept, woke up and made love again. Joe woke at daylight, dressed and kissed her goodbye, then went in his house by the front door with the key. Sam had locked the back door. Joe wondered if he had looked into his bedroom—he thought not. He felt at peace with the world. It was so good to be with Molly—he didn't dare think of the future if she should decide to go to England too. Dear God, how would he live without her? How could he go back to the loneliness of Kathleen—they were almost strangers now. 'Please God,' he prayed, 'let us stay together for ever.'

Kathleen came back after two days. She was looking better, Joe thought. Sam went off to work very happily each morning—he liked the work and his work mates, telling all the news of his day while he ate his evening meal. He went out in the evenings sometimes, and at other times he gave Joe a hand in the garden. Joe was proud of him— he was tall for his age and very handsome.

Cassie wrote to Molly every week, and sometimes enclosed a letter for Sam. Kathleen wondered what he did with the letters he got—she had searched his room, but couldn't find them. Actually Sam had put them into a large envelope and asked Molly to keep them for him. He was making a box at work during his lunch time—a box with a lock and key. When he'd finished, he brought it home, put the letters into it and locked it. Whenever he got a letter Joe always asked him how Cassie was, and Sam would tell him some of what she had written. Kathleen never asked—a fact that hurt Molly, who was always interested in Sam.

• • •

In October nineteen twenty nine, Johnny Scarlett was worried about his mother. He had always found his clothes washed and his food cooked, whatever time he got home, but she didn't seem to know day from night. He came in at two thirty one morning and found her cooking a dinner. On another occasion she had peeled potatoes, prepared cabbage and put them on the stove, but hadn't lit the fire under them. He went to see Eleanor, but got little sympathy from her. She said if Mother had a few cows to milk or chickens to feed, she would have been alright, but Johnny had sold off the cattle and poultry and poor Jane didn't know what to do with her time. Losing Father had been a terrible blow to her, and losing her daily routine just finished her.

"It's your fault, Johnny—you are idle and selfish, and now you come to me with six children and a home to run and you expect me to put it right. I'll write to Kathleen and Anna and between us we will help Mother—you will have to see to yourself."

So between the three sisters they worked out a rota: Kathleen came and stayed the first week, Anna came the second, and on the third week Eleanor came down each day with her baby after she had got the other children off to school—she couldn't stay overnight, but arranged for a neighbour to sleep there. It was hard work for them all, but Jane was better with one of her daughters there—she sometimes got their names mixed, but she was fed and warm and clean, and so dearly loved by them all.

It was Eleanor's turn to look after Jane. Johnny was about all day and he said he would be there all evening and night, so the neighbour was told she needn't come in. Eleanor hoped he was turning over a new leaf—he was very attentive to his mother, and when Eleanor went home she told Thomas that she thought Johnny was having a change for the better.

But at six o'clock next morning they were woken by a knock at the door—it was Johnny. He said he'd got up to see if Jane was alright and had found her dead. He had called the doctor, and he had said it was probably a heart attack. He'd sent someone to tell Anna and Kathleen.

Eleanor was stunned. And she also had a nagging doubt somewhere in her mind. What had Johnny done? His story didn't convince her. Her lovely mother dead? It was a nightmare.

She saw to her family then went down to the old home. Neighbours had come in, made tea and brought food. They were all so kind—Jane was loved by everyone. Each one could remember some kindness or help she had given to them. Kathleen arrived and took over, then Anna came. They all went into Jane's room where she was laid out, looking so peaceful, all the lines in her face gone. The three sisters cried together and hugged each other.

Robert and Eileen arrived later in the day. Robert was heartbroken. He adored his mother, and had always been proud of his parents. Their love for all their children and for each other had been a guiding light to him all his life, and now he lived by their standards and was given the respect himself that his father had always enjoyed.

Organising the funeral, following her coffin to the church and watching the burial tore at his heart. He tried to comfort his sisters, especially Eleanor. He still thought of her as his baby sister—she was eight years his junior. It seemed hard to believe that she was a mother of six, and she was the bravest of all his sisters.

He had a serious talk with his brother Johnny, who was taking his mothers death as he took everything. He asked Robert if he was going to share the funeral expenses.

"Mother had plenty of money," said Robert.

"Not any more," Johnny replied.

Robert looked at his brother with disgust. "I will pay the expenses, and I hope I never see you again."

Johnny just shrugged his shoulders and left the house.

The day after the funeral, Eleanor went down to say goodbye to Anna and Kathleen who had stayed the night. When she went in she found Robert in the kitchen alone.

"Where is everyone?" she asked.

Robert put the kettle on and said, "Eileen has gone over to see her parents; Anna and Kathleen are in the dining room, grabbing everything and fighting over it."

Eleanor went through to see them. There were two large boxes on the dining room table, and the two sisters were emptying the glass cabinet. Jane's lovely bone china and dinner service were on the table.

"What are you doing?" Eleanor was bewildered.

"I know mother wanted me to have the dinner service," Kathleen replied, "but Anna says she gave it to her."

They started arguing, and Eleanor came out of the room. Robert had made tea and handed her a cup.

Eleanor wept. "Robert, please stop them."

"I've tried," he said, "I'm ashamed of them. They haven't given you a thought, Sis. They've been in there all morning shouting at each other like fish wives.

"I think I'll go home," she said. "Poor mother would be horrified listening to those two. I won't go in there again, I couldn't stand it."

"I'll take you," said Robert, and he walked behind her out to the car. Before she got in he put a coat around her shoulders. She touched it and gasped, "This is mothers fur coat."

"It is," Robert replied, "and you shall have it. I took it out of her wardrobe this morning while they were fighting."

Eleanor pulled it round her—she could smell the Devon Violet perfume her mother used, and buried her nose in the soft fur.

"Robert," she said, "perhaps Eileen would like this."

He smiled at her. "Eileen has a fur coat—you take it. If they are looking for it, tell them I took it. If we leave it here they will pull it apart."

They sat together in the car. Eleanor said, "Do you remember Ladies night at the Masons? Mother in her dark red velvet dress, her lovely hair plaited in a coronet on top of her head and her black shoes with sparkling buckles."

"Yes," said Robert, "and father in evening dress, and he put on the little leather apron and you asked him if he had to cook dinner. He loved Lodge night, and he was so proud of mother—she looked so graceful, but she was a lady, no doubt about it."

Eleanor started to laugh and said, "Won't we look a sight at church on Sunday—Thomas in his ten year old suit, six shabby children and me in a fur coat."

"Thomas and the children are fine, and so are you. You've got a family to be proud of, and in case you want to dress them up, take this—spend it as you will." He put twenty pounds in Eleanor's hand.

"No Robert, we are not charity cases yet."

"I know you're not—you behaved as mother would have done today. You and I, Sis, are two of a kind. I will always be there for you if you want me," and he leaned over and kissed her.

Back in the dining room, Anna and Kathleen were still shouting at each other. They nearly came to blows over Jane's silver tea pot—in the end Anna got it, picked up her box and went off without saying goodbye. Robert left to pick Eileen up after he had dropped Eleanor off. He had taken nothing from the house, and cast a last look as he drove away. He wanted to remember it as it used to be, but already with the silence outside and his sisters quarrelling inside, he knew the rot had set in.

• • •

Kathleen arrived back late in the afternoon. She had taken a hired car from the station and was still fuming at Anna. She had wanted that teapot. She cooked an evening meal and was still in a temper.

"I'm the eldest," she grumbled, "I should have first pick. Father bought that teapot for mother for their tenth wedding anniversary, and it should have come to me."

Sam stopped eating and said, "Do you really need a silver teapot? There's nothing wrong with the one we've got."

Joe tried not laugh.

"That's not the point," Kathleen snapped, "what does she want with it either?"

"Well," Joe said, "by the look of that box you seem to have done all right. What did Eleanor get?"

Kathleen stopped eating. "I don't know," she said, "she just looked in and then went home."

"Poor little Auntie Eleanor," said Sam, "I'll bet she was so upset losing Grandma she didn't want anything."

Kathleen said no more. They hadn't offered Eleanor anything— she was the poorest of them all and they had forgotten her. All they had thought about was themselves. Poor little Eleanor, who had seen her mother most days, now had no one to turn to, and they had let her down. Kathleen pushed her chair back and ran upstairs she threw herself on the bed and wept tears of shame. What was happening to her? She had lost Sam's love and respect, and now she had lost Eleanor's, probably Robert's too. He had just nodded a curt goodbye. She doubted if Anna would be writing to her either. She had isolated herself from everyone. God help me she prayed—but it didn't help.

• • •

Johnny Scarlett was feeling isolated too. He was glad when everyone had gone and he had his house to himself at last. He stoked the fire and cooked himself bacon and eggs. There was a lot of food left after the funeral. He sat by the fire and dozed, then, waking up, decided to go to bed.

He looked around his bedroom with distaste. The sheets hadn't been changed for ages—Eleanor had stuck to her word and let him look after himself. He went into his mother's bedroom where his sisters had put clean sheets and pillow cases on—it looked nice. He went back to his own room and got into bed, but he was haunted by memories of his parents—his father trying to reason with him about drinking and gambling, his mother's care of him and her love which was always there. They had never deserted him, and he knew he had let them down time and time again.

At last he slept, but it was a troubled sleep. He woke at six thirty and decided to get up, going to the chest of drawers to get a clean shirt. He found the drawers were empty, sat on the side of his bed and wondered what to do next. There was a pile of dirty shirts on the floor, and at last he picked up the one that looked the cleanest, dressed and went downstairs. The big range seemed to stare back at him, cold and empty. He took out the ashes, lit the fire, put the kettle on and the frying pan. There was plenty of bacon and eggs and bread, but only a small piece of butter. He realised he would have to do some shopping, and what about his washing?

At last he decided to make peace with Eleanor. He would talk to her—she might help him out—and arrived at McMahon's just when they had finished their midday meal. Jeannie went out, and Thomas and Eleanor waited for him to speak..

"I wondered if you would like mother's dressing table," he began.

Eleanor looked at him. "And what do you want in return?" she asked.

"Would you do my laundry for me each week?"

Eleanor sat and sipped her tea. Let him sweat, she thought. After a while she said, "I'd love mother's dressing table, thank you Johnny. I'll do your laundry each week if you bring it here, and it will cost you ten shillings each week. If you leave it for two weeks it will be a pound."

Thomas opened his mouth to speak, but a look from Eleanor silenced him.

Johnny waited a moment. "That's a bit steep—what about five shillings per week?"

Eleanor put her hands on her hips. "I don't want to do your laundry at all," she said, "but if you want me to do it, it's ten shillings per week—take it or leave it."

"Alright," Johnny said, "ten shillings it is." He turned to Thomas. "Could you bring the milk dray down this evening? We could lay the dressing table flat on that—bring a blanket or some sacking to roll around it, to save damaging it." He got up to go. "Goodbye, Eleanor and thank you. I will see you this evening Thomas."

Thomas walked out with him. "Ten shillings seems a lot," Thomas said.

Johnny smiled. "Don't worry about it," he said, "I think there's some of me in Eleanor, after all."

Thomas came back into the house, and Eleanor waited for him to speak.

"I never thought I'd see the day that you would make deals with your family," he began.

"Nor did I," she replied, "but look at it this way—that's ten shillings he won't be able to spend on drink or on the horses he backs. I'll make better use of it. I knew he would come looking for help—he never could look after himself. He's so lazy, I dread to think what the house will be like, but I'm not doing his cleaning and cooking—I've got enough to do here, as you very well know."

Thomas put his arms around her. "I think you are a great wife and mother," he said, "and I love you Ely. Even with six children you are still the pick of the bunch."

"You're not so bad yourself, Thomas, and I love you too," she said.

• • •

While Kathleen had been going up to look after her mother, Joe and Molly had been working like slaves. Molly had planned to make the cakes for the Saturday stall on Thursday and Friday, but the Doctor had called and asked her to deliver a baby in one of the local cottages and again on Friday morning.

"Where's the district nurse?" Molly asked him.

"She's up at the Manse—there's a baby due there too," he replied.

Molly smiled to herself. The Manse for the District Nurse and the cottages for Molly, she thought. But Molly liked the cottages best—she had grown up in the area and everyone knew her.

When she went into the Kennedy's cottage, there were three children in the kitchen, two washing up and one being a nuisance.

"Hello, where's Mam?" said Molly.

"Upstairs—Mrs Johnston's with her," replied the eldest.

Molly went up, and both women smiled. "Hello Molly, thank goodness it's you."

"How are the pains, Bridget?"

"Every twenty minutes."

"I'll just make up the fire and put the kettles on," Molly said. "You'll be alright for a while."

She helped the children tidy the kitchen, found a kettle boiling, and made a cup of tea for the two women upstairs and for herself. She asked the children if they'd had breakfast, and they said yes.

"If you want to go and play you can then," Molly told them, and they were gone like a shot.

Mrs Kennedy had a baby boy at three o'clock that afternoon. Molly did what was needed and gave the children their tea, then she cooked a meal for Pat Kennedy when he came home from work, and it was nearly six o'clock when she got home. She baked some cakes, and sat down at ten o'clock dead tired.

Joe came round. "You looked whacked Molly."

"I am," she said. "I seem to be called out more often just lately, but I don't want to give up the midwifery—I love it."

"I've been thinking," said Joe, "I really need a man full time now. I've put a note in the post office window—the garden has grown too big. I really wanted to keep it small and manage it myself, but it's got busier every week."

"I think that's a good idea, and I don't want to let you down either, Joe—you've given me a lease on life."

Joe hugged her. She was so tired she fell asleep in his arms, and Joe dozed off too—he had had a busy day and hadn't finished everything. Molly woke up at midnight. "Joe," she whispered, "you had better go home, or Sam will lock you out."

"It's alright," Joe replied, "I've got the front door key—let's go to bed."

He got up at five o'clock, made Molly a cup of tea and went home. There he lit his fire, called Sam, and they ate breakfast together.

"I wonder how long mother's going to have to go up to Scarlett's," Sam said.

"As long as it takes," Joe said. "Jane has got very frail, but she could go on for years."

"I don't think she will," Sam said, "she's been different ever since Grandad died. I don't think she wants to live."

The very next day a young man called about the job. Joe liked the look of him—he was twenty eight years old, lived a mile away and he had a wife and baby. They had just moved down from Dublin—he had worked in the linen mills, but had been paid off. Joe decided to give him a try, and found that he worked hard—it made a world of difference having another pair of hands.

Molly was called out again on Friday—she wondered if she was ever going to get the bread made for the stall. She got home at eight o'clock in the evening, decided to go to bed, set the alarm clock for four, and had everything ready by nine thirty. She hoped she wouldn't be called out on Saturday. Luckily she sold out early on the stall, she went home and fell asleep on the sofa. When Joe came in at four thirty in the afternoon she was still asleep, so he crept out again and left her.

• • •

Sam Lyons had just had his seventeenth birthday. He was a tall, good looking young man, as tall as his father. He still worked for Preston Timbers and could do any job that came along. His father had two full-time men helping in the gardens, and everything was going well. Sam talked to Kathleen, but was cautious what he told her. She was still possessive and would have interfered, so he was polite, talked a little about his work, but never mentioned what he did in his spare time.

Cassie had been home twice, for six weeks each year, and was now very good-looking. She and Sam had gone out for a picnic on their bikes to the top of Monument Hill. They had always been able to talk to each other, and she told him she hoped to go into nursing, like Molly had.

"Where will you go to train?" Sam asked.

"I've put my name down at St Thomas's in London," she said. "It's a good hospital—two of my friends have put their names down as well, so after my eighteenth birthday I'll hope to start.

Eleanor hadn't heard from Kathleen or Anna since Jane's death. She missed hearing from them, but she was always busy, with poultry to look after, three cows to milk, her beehives to see to, as well as cooking, cleaning and washing for her large family. John and Harold were doing the milk drays now, and Thomas worked the land. It was summer time and things were easier financially, but she still worked from morning till night. And now she realised she was pregnant again.

It was nineteen thirty one—Bill was four and Jessica was eight. Bill would be at school next year, so it wouldn't be too bad, but she often felt tired and went to bed very early.

One Sunday, she got a surprise when Joe and Sam Lyons walked in, having cycled all the way over. She hadn't seen them for two years. Joe looked well, Sam was a grown man, and all the McMahon children were delighted to see them. Jessica took Joe's hand and said she had a surprise for him.

In the corner of the barn lay Tess, the sheep dog, with six puppies, cream and white like Tess—little bundles of fur, playing and rolling around.

"How old are they?" Joe asked.

"Nine weeks," said Jessica, as she picked one up. "This is my favourite—I call her Cassie. They'll all be going soon—I want to keep this one, but I'm not sure if I can."

Thomas came into the barn. "A good litter Joe."

"They're beautiful," Joe said, "all spoken for, I suppose."

"Four are—the four dogs—the two bitches are not."

Joe picked up the other bitch and showed it to Sam. "Do you think Molly would like her?"

"Funny you should say that," Sam replied. "Cassie told me the other day Molly would like a dog for company."

"I'll take it then," said Joe. "But how are we going to get it home?"

Eleanor found a basket with a lid and put a piece of blanket in it. "If you tie that securely on the back of your bike, it should be alright," she said.

"Is it alright to take it today?"

"Yes, they're all eating now and drinking from a dish—poor Tess is nearly dry. Thomas thinks we might keep the other bitch—Tess is eight years old now, and past her prime."

Joe winked at Jessica, "Well that's settled then. What do I owe you?"

"Not a penny," said Thomas, "you're welcome to it."

"I'd rather pay," Joe insisted.

"Nonsense," said Eleanor, "we're glad to get rid of it—the dogs are going this week."

When they were leaving, Joe kissed Eleanor. "I hear there's a new baby on the way." He put five pound into her hand. "Buy it something from me."

"There's no need," Joe" she said.

"I know that, but it would please me for you to take it—I wish we were having a new baby, but there's not much chance of that."

"Poor Joe," said Eleanor hugging him, "you deserve better."

The puppy cried for a while in the basket, but then went to sleep, and Joe and Sam rode along talking.

"There's a girl who works in the outfitters in Enniskillen," Sam said. "We eat our sandwiches together in the park."

"What's she like?" Joe asked.

"Well she's tall and she has fair hair cut quite short and she's got blue eyes—she can be funny sometimes, we have a good laugh. She can mimic the manageress—you'd think it was the manageress, she does it so well. She's asked me home to tea next Sunday—do you think I should tell mother?"

"Yes—tell her a young lady has asked you home to tea, but don't let her talk you out of it. I think she gets a bit jealous sometimes. Perhaps you could ask her home to tea with us—I'd like to meet her."

"I'll see how it goes on Sunday first," Sam replied.

When they got home, Sam carried the puppy in to show Kathleen.

"I don't really want a dog," She said

Sam replied, "It's not for us, it's for Molly—she gets lonely without Cassie."

Molly was sitting on the garden bench when he brought it round and put it into her arms.

"What a lovely present, Sam," said Molly cuddling it. "She's very sweet—what shall I call her?"

"I'm not much good with names," he laughed.

"I think I'll call her Candy," Molly said, "she's as sweet as candy."

"That's a good name for her," Sam said, "Candy Peters."

Molly sat with the sleeping puppy on her lap. The little dog was great fun—lollaping around the garden, biting Molly's bare toes or swinging on the hem of her dress. She had made a bed for it in a clothes basket with some old jumpers of Cassie's, and had put a stone hot water bottle in, and it had settled down and was still sleeping when she came down at five thirty in the morning.

• • •

Joe told Kathleen that Eleanor was expecting again.

"You should go and see her, or write to her at least. It's ridiculous sisters falling out—you were all so close once. Your mother would be horrified if she knew, and I expect she does know."

"I will," Kathleen said. "I'll write to her and Anna. You're right Joe—we should never have quarrelled. I'll start knitting for her too."

"And you could get your sewing machine out and make the baby a few clothes. I don't think she has time—she never sits down."

Kathleen was as good as her word. She wrote Eleanor a long, loving letter, said she would make whatever baby clothes was needed, and that she would come and look after the family during the confinement. She also wrote to Anna, told her Eleanor was pregnant and hoped Anna would try and get to see her.

Eleanor felt better that she'd had a letter from both her sisters. It was good to be on friendly terms again—she tried to forget the time Jane had died and the bitter quarrel between them, and she was glad she'd had no part in it. On reflection, she had a lovely fur coat and her dear mother's dressing table, and she had asked for nothing. She wondered how Kathleen would react when she saw the dressing table.

Kathleen arrived on the fourth of December. The baby was due, and Eleanor was weary. It had been a long, hot summer and she was glad it was a winter baby—there was no work in the fields until the peat cutting in March.

117

When Kathleen saw the dressing table, she stopped short. "How did you get that?"

Eleanor laughed, and explained about Johnny wanting his laundry done. "He asked me if I'd like the dressing table just to sweeten me up—I said I'd love it. He didn't expect me to charge him ten shillings per week for his laundry, but I said take it or leave it, that's the price."

"Does he pay it?" Kathleen asked.

"He has to give me the money when he brings the washing—if he hasn't got ten shillings he can take the dirty laundry back with him—I don't play games."

Kathleen couldn't help laughing. "I'll bet he's sorry he gave it away."

"No," Eleanor said, "I think he couldn't bear to look at it. He's still feeling guilty about the way he treated Mother and Father—he was always a worry to them, and I expect the house is in a right pickle. I haven't been down to see it for ages—I haven't been well enough to walk that far. I believe he sleeps in mother's room now—it's always double sheets to wash—but the house is his, and he can sleep where he likes. I don't think he sleeps alone either—I've heard tales about a Mrs Morrison who's husband died a while back. I think she spends a lot of time with Johnny."

"It's a pity she doesn't do his washing then."

"What and take away my income?" Eleanor laughed. "No, I think Mrs M has other things to do when she's with Johnny."

"Disgusting!" declared Kathleen.

Eleanor had a baby boy on December the seventh, nineteen thirty one. He was a small baby, five and half pounds in weight. Eleanor wasn't well afterwards—it was the first time she'd had a doctor with her during a birth, but the nurse insisted and the doctor told Thomas, 'no more babies, and no more work in the fields for at least a year.'

Thomas was worried. Eleanor was always strong and well, and he never asked her to work in the fields, but she could work as well as any man and he had been glad of her help. It was a blessing that John and Harold were old enough to give a hand.

Anna came to see Eleanor and brought clothes for all the little ones. She stayed a week, and she and Kathleen were friends.

Joe and Sam looked after themselves. Molly cooked their evening meal each day, and Joe slipped round late at night and slept there until daylight.

Sam was busy seeing his girlfriend. They visited each other every weekend—her name was Jenny Gray, and Joe liked her. She was a big girl, long legs and wide shoulders, and very easy to talk to. Kathleen had been to the shop where she worked to buy material and wool for Eleanor's baby, and couldn't find any fault with her—but she thought Sam was besotted with her, and it made her angry. She told Eleanor and Anna that she thought Jenny was bold and that she was trying to trap Sam. They both knew how she felt about Sam, so they said nothing.

One day Kathleen was hanging up Eleanor's dressing gown in the wardrobe and saw the fur coat. Anna was sitting with Jessica on her lap at the edge of Eleanor's bed.

"Oh look," cried Kathleen, "it's mothers fur coat."

Poor Eleanor felt guilty, but Jessica said, "Uncle Robert gave it to Mammie—he was afraid you and Aunt Anna would tear it in half."

Kathleen and Eleanor laughed, and Anna said, "That was a bit underhand, but I'm surprised he didn't take it for Eileen.",

"Auntie Eileen already had a fur coat," said Jessica, "and Mammie loves that one, don't you Mammie?"

• • •

Sam took Jenny round to meet Molly, and they took to each other straight away. Jenny fell in love with Candy—Molly had bought a collar and lead, and Sam and Jenny took her over the fields. She was a beautiful dog, and Molly's gentle handling had produced an obedient little animal. Her only fear was that Candy, being a working dog, hadn't any work to do in the cottage and garden, so she started to take her on the farm morning and evenings, where she rounded up the cows for milking and helped to put the ducks and geese to bed. Fred would have liked to have kept her, but Molly said she was a gift from Sam and she couldn't give her away—besides she loved her company. If she went upstairs she found Candy waiting at the bottom, and when she came down again she sat and watched while Molly hung the washing out or worked in the garden.

"What do you think of Jenny?" Joe asked Molly one day.

"I like her," replied Molly. "She's handsome, wholesome and un-complicated."

"That describes her exactly," Joe laughed "and besides, she's good for Sam."

"I wonder how she and Cassie will get along," Molly said. "They are very alike really."

"Except that Cassie is beautiful as well as wholesome and uncom-plicated."

"Well beauty, they say, is only skin deep," Molly answered. "How does she and Kathleen get on, or shouldn't I ask?"

"You know Kathleen," Joe said. "Whoever Sam is with would never be good enough in Kathleen's eyes. If only she knew how much he dislikes her—it's unnatural—mother and son should love each other."

Molly was out of her depth here. "It's as though she's in love with her own son."

"That just about sums it up," Joe said sadly, "and the trouble is all her own making. She's bitter and difficult, and sometimes I feel like running away—and I would if you weren't next door."

Molly was troubled. She'd known for a long time that Joe and Kathleen slept apart, but she hadn't realised how unhappy Joe was. She was glad that they loved each other. She used to feel guilty about it, but not now—they needed each other, and they were hurting no-one.

• • •

Cassie had completed two years training at St Thomas's Hospital, and came home for two weeks. She had been a good student and passed her exams with honours—twenty years old and as lovely as ever.

Joe teased her: "I'll bet all the young doctors are crazy about you."

Cassie laughed: "They're crazy about anything in a nurses uniform. The place is crawling with lovely girls—blondes, brunettes and redheads. We all work hard, and when we get a bit of free time we all go out and enjoy ourselves. The next two years will be hard, but I take each day as it comes."

Cassie met Jenny and they were soon chatting like old friends. Joe wondered if Jenny would be jealous, but if she was it didn't show. Kathleen hoped there would be trouble between them, but it didn't happen. Cassie had actually felt a twinge of jealousy, but she would soon be on her way back to London, plenty of work and good friends, and she told herself to be glad for Sam. Jenny was a nice girl and Sam deserved her, bless him. She had caught a look between Joe and her mother, and wondered if they were lovers. A lot of things this holiday had made her think that Molly was like the cat who'd got the cream—well Joe and Molly deserved a bit of happiness too. Cassie was broadminded now, after two years in London.

Sam had just had his twenty-second birthday, and he and Jenny were going to get engaged. He told Joe and Kathleen.

"Congratulations son," and Joe, "when are you getting married?"

"Not for a couple of years—I want to buy a house, nothing grand, just a small one to start."

"I'll help you out, Sam," Joe said. I've put a bit aside and you're welcome to it."

"No dad," he replied, "we'll try to go it on our own. You've worked hard for your money, and we can work hard too."

When Sam left, Kathleen rounded on Joe.

"What do you think you're doing, offering our savings?"

"What the hell do you mean *our* savings? It's *my* savings, Kathleen, every penny of it. You would still be in Archdale sewing. I'm the one who slaved for this place. Sam is my son, and he can have the lot. I hope he gets married and has a half dozen children—I wish I had."

"You know I couldn't have any more children," Kathleen had tears in her eyes.

"Couldn't? Wouldn't you mean. You wanted a wedding ring and a child. Well, you got that. You hardly noticed me except on pay night, and you spoiled Sam's childhood. Now don't try any tricks, my girl, because I'll be watching you."

"You sound like you hate me," Kathleen was crying now.

"I don't hate anyone—I just don't like you any more. But we're married, so I suppose we'll have to stay together. I'll provide for us both, and you do the house keeping—but if you ever want to move out, feel free."

Kathleen was stunned. Did Joe mean it? She knew he meant it. She asked herself, could she leave him? She knew she could if she had anywhere to go—but Sam? That was different—she couldn't bear the thought of not seeing him. He was the core of her life. She couldn't bear the thought of him and Jenny sleeping together and having children. Her head felt like it was going to burst, her hands shook and she felt giddy. How could she stop the marriage?

Next day she went into the shop where Jenny worked and selected a few things—some needles, elastic, a couple of spools of cotton thread—and handed Jenny a five pound note. The goods came to seven shillings and six pence. Jenny handed her the change. Kathleen walked to the door and turned.

"I think you have short-changed me," she said.

"I don't think so," Jenny said. "Four pound twelve shillings and six pence."

"But I gave you ten pounds."

"No," Jenny said, "it was five pounds."

"I want to see the manageress," Kathleen said.

So the manageress was called. "What's the trouble?" she asked.

"This girl gave me change for five pounds—I gave her ten pounds."

The manageress opened the till, and there was no ten pound note in there—only a five pound. She had taken the notes out only a few minutes before, and was on the way to the bank when Kathleen had started to fuss.

"I'm sorry, madam," she said, "there isn't a ten pound note in here. Jenny never makes mistakes—I wouldn't keep her here if she wasn't totally honest and good with figures."

Kathleen had to back down, say she was sorry and leave the shop. Jenny was puzzled. Why had Sam's mother done it—did she want to get her sacked or what?

Kathleen knew she had made a mistake. In trying to discredit Jenny, she had discredited herself. Jenny would tell Sam, and Sam would tell Joe—where would it end?

Jenny didn't tell Sam, but she did tell Molly when she came into the shop a couple of days later. Business was slow that day, Jenny was alone in the shop and Molly sat down and talked. She told Jenny how possessive Kathleen was where Sam was concerned, but she advised her to try not to have a row—it would be hard on Sam and Joe, and perhaps Kathleen would come to accept that Sam was now a man and could make his own decisions.

Jenny had to force herself to visit on Sundays, and usually went round to Molly's as soon as she could. She and Sam didn't talk to Kathleen about their plans. They were saving every penny they could—then Jenny's grandfather died and left her a hundred pounds, so they arranged a wedding date.

Kathleen changed tactics. Sam came down from his room dressed to go out, and Joe thought how smart he looked—grey trousers and a Harris Tweed jacket, pale blue shirt and tie—but Kathleen frowned and said, "It's time you bought yourself some decent clothes, Sam—you're beginning to look shabby."

Sam laughed. "These will last a while yet. I've got better things to do with my money."

"You're socks are all in holes," snapped Kathleen.

"Jenny will darn them for me," Sam said, "she's a dab hand with a needle," and he went out.

Kathleen said, "I can't imagine her darning socks."

"Can't you?" said Joe. "I think she will be a great wife for him, and I'm looking forward to having grandchildren."

• • •

The wedding was on a Saturday. Kathleen didn't want to go, but Joe was firm.

"You will dress in your best," he told her, "and we will watch our son being married, and you will be nice to Jenny's parents and do nothing to spoil their day."

Joe wondered how he was going to cope with her when Sam had left. He hadn't been round to Molly's for ages—he needed her, her warmth, her soft voice and above all her wonderful body—Oh dear God, how he needed her. Just seeing her and her dog in her garden made him want to jump over the fence and carry her away.

Kathleen behaved politely at the wedding. She had taken a lot of trouble with her appearance, and looked smart. She kissed Jenny's cheek at the reception, and talked a little to Jenny's parents. Then, during the speeches Joe stood up, put his arms around Jenny and Sam and said, "This is a wonderful day for my wife and I. I give Jenny a hearty welcome into our family. She is a lovely girl, we love her already, and I think Sam is a very lucky man—so let's drink to their happiness, good health and long life."

After the meal was over and cleared away, some musicians arrived and Sam and Jenny danced slowly in each others arms. Soon they were joined by Joe and Kathleen and Jenny's parents, then they swapped partners—Jenny danced with the best man and Sam danced with the bridesmaid, then he danced with Molly. Some time later Joe danced with Molly. They spun slowly around, almost cheek to cheek.

Jenny nudged Sam, "Look at your Dad and Molly," she whispered.

"I know," he replied, "I've often wondered about them, but I will say this, I don't blame him—my mother is impossible, I don't know how he stands it. I've had a lot of love from Molly and Cassie—I could tell them anything and they always understood."

On the dance floor Joe and Molly had forgotten everyone except themselves.

"It's been a long time, Joe," she said.

"Far too long," he answered, "what are we going to do about it?" They knew there wasn't much they could do. "I'd like to pick you up right now and carry you away and never come back," he said.

Molly smiled. "What a scandal that would create."

The music stopped and they parted. Kathleen had been watching them too, and when Joe sat down beside her she whispered at him furiously, "That was quite an exhibition—did you have to hold her so tightly? or was it her idea."

"It was a joint decision," Joe snapped. He got up and went over to Sam and Jenny.

"Mother looks miffed," Sam said.

"I think I was unwise to dance with Molly," his father answered.

Sam patted his shoulder. "Enjoy yourself dad—have another dance. You'll still catch it when you get home and she won't speak to Molly for a month, you wait and see. It's a shame Cassie couldn't get over for today—she would have enjoyed herself. Molly was telling me she's learned to drive, and her grandfather has bought her a little car—an Austin seven. I can picture her flying round Hindhead frightening the locals."

"She's a great girl," Joe said, "and she's a credit to her mother."

• • •

The wedding was over, and everything was back to normal. Joe thought how quiet the house was—not peaceful quiet, but empty quiet. Sam had cleared out his room—nothing but furniture in there now. Kathleen didn't talk much, but Joe noticed the sewing machine was out on the sitting room table. He was glad to see that she was busy—although he didn't love her, he would have liked to see her happy—happy and busy like she used to be.

He asked her what she was making, and she said she'd found some material which she had forgotten about and she was making clothes for the Kennedy children.

"Bridget Kennedy was in the Post Office the other day, and she was saying what a struggle it was, dressing four of them. I think her husband drinks a lot of his wages, but they say he is a good worker. Anyway, I've enough for a dress each for the girls, and there's some of Sam's old things in the loft. I may be able to alter them. Do you want a cup of tea," Kathleen added.

"Yes," he replied, "but you carry on sewing—I'll make us both a cup.

Making the tea, Joe thought at least they were talking to each other, and perhaps helping the Kennedy's would cheer her up. Waiting to the kettle to boil, he looked down the garden. Molly and Candy were working—at least, Molly was trying to work, but Candy kept bringing a stick for her to throw. Molly raised her arm and the stick went far out into the back field. The little dog raced after it and disappeared into the hedge. Molly looked round and saw Joe at the window. She waved, and he waved back. There and then, he decided to go round to her cottage after supper.

"I'm going for a walk," he said to Kathleen.

"At ten o'clock at night?"

"It's the best time of the day," he replied.

He walked up the road. It was quiet and peaceful, and when he came back he saw Molly's light was on in the kitchen. He opened the back door and went in. Molly was sitting at the range reading, the dog on her lap.

"I had to come round," he said. "I couldn't stay away any longer."

"I'm glad you did." She smiled at him. "I was lonely thinking of Cassie and Sam both flown the nest, and I was wondering where you, Kathleen and I were heading. But let's make the best of our time. Come on up to bed—I feel reckless tonight."

They made love tenderly and slowly, and went to sleep. Joe woke at one o'clock in the morning, dressed and slipped away without waking her up. Candy wagged her tail at him as he went out. He let himself into his house, locked the back door and went up to bed—he wondered if Kathleen was asleep, but he didn't really care. He was happy, unbelievably happy, and he went to sleep at once.

At six in the morning when he came down the stairs, he found Kathleen up and sitting with a cup of tea. "I didn't hear you come in," she said.

"I tried to come quietly in case I woke you."

"Did you enjoy your walk?" she asked.

"I did indeed—thoroughly enjoyed it, and I mean to do it oftener."

So it became a pattern of their lives. Once or twice a week, Joe went round to Molly and Kathleen went to bed. She wasn't entirely happy about these late night walks, but she didn't think he was with Molly—she thought he was at the local public house, and she said so to Molly one day.

"Joe has taken to going out a couple of nights each week—I wonder if he's started drinking."

Molly didn't know where to look, but said, "Joe has never struck me as a drinking man. I think he misses Sam and likes to get away by himself."

Kathleen laughed. "I miss Sam too, but I don't intend to walk the roads at midnight," she said.

125

Sam and Jenny dropped in on their first wedding anniversary and announced that Jenny was pregnant. They were very happy, and Joe was delighted.

"That's the best news I've heard in a long time. Now you take care of yourself Jenny, and if you need anything you have only to ask."

"Oh we have all we need," Jenny said. "But I must go round and see Molly—I saw her at the doctor's this morning. I hope she's alright—I thought she looked pale."

Joe's heart missed a beat. Molly ill? He wouldn't even think about it.

Jenny came back a little later. "Is she alright?" Sam asked.

"She says her back aches and her right leg is painful too. The Doctor gave her some tablets, and she's sitting with her feet up—I've never seen her do that before."

As soon as they left, Joe said to Kathleen, "I'll go round and see if Molly needs anything. She should tell us if she's not well. Hearing about the baby will cheer her up."

In her kitchen he looked at her sitting with her feet on a stool. He was anxious. "Molly love, what's wrong?"

"It's just backache. It will be alright in a day or two—there is no need to fuss."

"Why didn't you tell me? You know I'm always here—now have you had any tea?"

"Yes, thank you, I've had tea and toast, but I wasn't very hungry." She smiled at him. "You are fussing over nothing—I'll be fine."

Joe made up the fire, fed the dog and took it for a walk. When he came back, Molly said she was going to bed, and made her way painfully towards the stairs. Joe helped her up, saw her into bed, then kissed her and held her.

"Just knock the wall and I'll be round if you need anything."

"I will," she said, "and don't worry—Goodnight Joe."

"Goodnight my dearest," he said and left.

Next morning he took Candy up to the farm. Molly said her back was a bit better, but her leg was numb. She had got up, lit her fire and had breakfast, but she didn't feel up to walking to the farm. Joe told Fred he was worried. "I don't think she should be alone at night. If she fell down those narrow stairs she could kill herself."

Fred agreed. "I think I'll write to Cassie," he said. "Molly will skin me alive, but then Cassie will skin me alive if we don't tell her."

Joe felt better—perhaps Cassie could get a bit of time off. In the meantime, he and Kathleen would keep an eye on her. Kathleen went round, cleaned the cottage and made Molly a dinner. She also changed the sheet and took them home to wash. She could see Molly was in great pain, and she really wished she could help her—until Molly said, "Great news from Sam and Jenny—a baby on the way—I must write and tell Cassie."

Kathleen stared at her and rushed out of the house without saying a word. Molly sighed: "Now what have I done?"

Her back got a little better, but she limped when she walked, and the doctor advised her to go into hospital and see a specialist. He admitted he didn't know what was wrong—he thought it was a trapped nerve, and Molly said it felt like it. She was taking the tablets, but she knew they were just pain killers.

• • •

A week later a little car stopped outside the cottages and Cassie climbed out, stretched her arms and walked into the cottage. Molly was sitting with her feet up. "Cassie, where on earth have you sprung from?"

"I've just popped home for a holiday, so how about a hug?"

Molly got to her feet painfully and hugged her daughter.

Cassie looked at her. "I think you'd better explain why you are sitting with your feet up—you look terrible." Then in a softer voice, "What's wrong Mam?"

Molly explained and showed her the tablets.

"You need an X-ray," Cassie said firmly. "I don't think they do X-rays in Enniskillen—we'll have to go to Belfast and get it sorted out."

She made tea and afterwards fetched in her luggage, the little dog following her about. She bent down and stroked it. "I expected you to look after my Mam," she said, and the dog sat and offered her its paw. She shook it and said, "Don't worry, we'll get her put right."

The next day she drove Molly down to the Royal Victoria Hospital at Belfast in her car. She saw specialists and surgeons, and they decided to operate and find out what the trouble was. It was a tumour on the spinal column. They removed it, and after four weeks Molly was back home and on her feet again.

Cassie stayed at home another month. She was very reluctant to go, not liking the look of Molly at all. Sam and Jenny came to see her before she left, and they promised to keep an eye on her—if she wasn't getting better they would write and tell her. She also had a long talk with Joe. She could see how upset he was, and he told her how much Molly meant to him. She smiled and said she guessed that they loved each other.

"Are you angry with me Cassie?" Joe asked.

"Why should I be angry?" she laughed, "you are two lovely people. I think you were made for each other, but it couldn't be—but I've often wondered why all those years ago you stopped and asked Uncle Fred about the cottage."

Joe smiled. "Perhaps our guardian angels decided for us, but it's been great having her next door and seeing her every day, and just sometimes having a little while together. I feel I've been lucky—and having you as well, Cassie—you and Sam were great friends. You made a man of him—I had hoped you and he would marry."

"There was no question of that," Cassie said. "I loved him like a brother and I always will. I'm glad he's happy—Jenny is a lovely girl, and the baby coming too—he seems to have managed very well."

So Cassie went back to London. Molly missed her, but Joe looked in every morning and came and stayed a couple of hours every evening. Sam and Jenny called in regularly, and so things settled down.

Next door, Kathleen wasn't happy. She couldn't see why Joe wanted to sit with Molly each evening, and her tongue ran riot every night when he came in. She complained to Sam and everyone she met about it, but Joe just listened and said little. He knew if he started to argue with her he would probably end up by hitting her, and he didn't want to do that. He knew she was her own worst enemy, and if he sat in with her every night she would find something else to nag about.

Jenny had a baby girl. They brought it to show Kathleen and Joe, and then to Molly. She was a placid baby and slept well. They named her Jane Marie, and Joe was very happy for them, but when they left, Kathleen said she didn't think the baby looked at all like Sam, and added, "He probably isn't its father anyway."

Joe was livid. What a thing to say about their first grandchild. He lost his temper and called her a evil-minded bitch. They stopped speaking to each other, and Joe told Sam not to bring the baby for a while. He didn't explain why, but Sam guessed it was something Kathleen had said.

• • •

About a year later Molly started to have pains again, in her legs and arms. Joe wrote to Cassie and she came home again, this time having given up her job to stay with Molly for as long as she needed her. She drove her to Belfast again, and the specialist who examined her told Cassie the cancer had spread and he could only offer pain killers. He thought she might live about six months. Molly wanted to know what the specialist said, and Cassie told her the truth—Molly was a nurse herself and knew what to expect, and she was quite cheerful when they got back.

The stairs in the cottage were steep and narrow, and Cassie suggested bringing her single bed to the sitting room—it would be easier all round as it was difficult carrying trays up and down, and Molly could rest on the bed any time. So Sam and Joe carried the little bed downstairs and put it up in the sitting room. Joe brought in flowers to make the room cheerful, and Candy slept beside the bed. Molly did a little work when she felt like it, but she was often in pain and had no energy.

She looked forward to the evenings when Joe came round. Cassie went out to visit friends sometimes, and Molly didn't care what Kathleen thought—soon she could have Joe all to herself. All she wanted was Joe as often as possible, and she wondered how he would cope with her death. She looked at her arms, now so thin—even her shoes were too big for her—and she found it hard to keep warm. She only felt warm when Joe sat on the bed and held her in his arms.

Molly didn't live for six months. About three months after she had seen the specialist, she couldn't get out of bed and her mind started wandering. Cassie went out into the garden and told Joe. As he came through the door Molly held out her arms, and he held her until she died an hour later.

• • •

Everyone in the neighbourhood attended the funeral and the flowers were piled high—she was loved by all. Cassie had known what to expect, but no one had warned her about the emptiness. The cottage was dreary, and the little dog was fretting and wouldn't eat. She walked her up to the farm and Fred took her to fetch the cows. Seeing this brighten her up, Cassie asked him to keep her—he had always wanted her—and the dog settled down well with him. But then the cottage was quieter than ever, and Cassie decided to pack up and go back to her grandparents at Hindhead.

Joe said he was thinking of leaving too. He had no interest in the garden and no love in his home. He took a look in the papers each week, and one day saw an advertisement for an older man to look after

JESSICA'S PEOPLE

the Rectory garden and keep the churchyard tidy. There was a small flat free with the job—he applied, was interviewed, and got it.

That night as he and Kathleen sat having their tea, he told her he was moving out.

She looked at him in shock. "What about me?" she cried.

"You can stay here or move away, whatever you like. I will continue to support you financially, where ever you are."

"But where are you going?" Kathleen asked.

"Perhaps it's better if you don't know," Joe replied. "I'll arrange for your money to be at the Post Office every Friday."

"And what about the gardens?"

"Fred's son is taking over," said Joe. "We've talked about it. and I'll show him over this week—then he can do what he likes with it."

"You are giving it away? The greenhouses and the stock."

"No, I've arranged for him to pay me as he goes along."

"All this, and I wasn't consulted," she said bitterly.

"Kathleen," he replied reasonably, "when have you shown any interest in the garden?"

"I've had my stall every Saturday."

"Yes and you pocketed the takings each week, so you've done very well for yourself—and perhaps you can still have your stall, but you must arrange that yourself."

"I can't face people—they will all know you've left me."

"Then tell them why I left you," he answered, and left the room.

He gathered up his belongings—he didn't have much, just a couple of best suits, a few sweaters, socks, shoes and underwear. He looked out his gardening books, his Bible, and that was it. He decided to take his bicycle, as he loved the country side and would have more time now to look at it and enjoy it.

Kathleen was very much alone now. The cottage next door was empty. She noticed Molly's little dog in the garden sometimes, still looking for Molly, and she tried to make friends with it, but it ran off back to the farm. She got out her sewing machine and some material she'd bought and put away, but she couldn't settle down to doing anything. Her sister Anna wrote to her and asked her to come and stay awhile, so she went and stayed and she really didn't want to come back.

Anna advised her to make her peace with Sam and Jenny, and one day they went to see Eleanor and Thomas. Thomas was very feeble and had to be helped in and out of his chair. Eleanor had lost her bloom too, and had had a lot of worries. Her two eldest were in Eng-

130

land, Polly was away at work, and Bob was also working away from home. Jessica was starting work soon, and the two little boys were still at school.

Kathleen cried as she told them how Joe had left her, and Eleanor turned on her and said, "No wonder—you've led him a hell of a life, Kathleen—and where's your Sam now? Siding with Joe no doubt! You brought it all on yourself. Don't ever criticise Joe to me, he was a lovely boy and a fine man—you should have looked after him."

When she got back to her cottage Kathleen started sewing again. She looked out patterns and bought more material, and she worked on late into the night. She picked up her money each Friday from the Post Office and bought her food, but never stopped to talk to people. Children avoided her and ran to their mothers as she passed by—she had no friends. Sam came rarely, but they usually had an argument before he left, so his visits became even rarer.

Two years went by since Joe left, and one day the milkman found yesterday's milk still on the doorstep. He hurried to the Post Office and the Post Mistress got in touch with Sam. Kathleen had collapsed beside her sewing machine—she had had a stroke, and was rushed to hospital. Sam and Joe visited her there, but she kept her eyes closed all the time they were there, and two weeks later she died, alone except for the nurses. Her funeral was a quiet affair—just Joe and Sam, Anna and George, and Eleanor's daughter Polly.

Joe didn't want to go into the cottage—so many memories, good and bad, chased each other through his mind. He told Sam to take whatever he wanted, but Sam only took the looking glass with two roses entwined at the top of the frame.

"It's all I've got of my wonderful grandfather," he said sadly.

Joe sold the cottage with the contents and never went near the place again.

He went back to his little home and cried for poor Kathleen and for Molly, and at last he came to terms with Molly's death. He wished Kathleen had lived and learned to be happy—Molly's death had taken the heart out of him—and he suddenly remembered the big box of children's clothes he and Sam had found in the cottage. Kathleen had made coats, dresses, skirts, blouses, petticoats—at least thirty garments, all sitting by the sewing machine. Had she meant to give them to Jenny and end the long silence between them? But Jenny had said she didn't want the clothes, so Sam had taken them to the Orphanage where they were welcomed.

They would never know what Kathleen's intentions were. Joe often had a cup of tea with the rector, who was a widower, and they talked of many things. Joe had been good churchman and liked to hear a good sermon. He had many friends, but could also shut himself away in his little flat and read and dream.

He lived until he was eighty. Sam and Jenny spent a lot of time with him, and his grandchildren adored him. He left all his worldly goods to Sam, asking only to be buried in the churchyard he had looked after for so many years. And so ended the life and loves of a totally honest man.

Jessica

❧ ❧ ❧

Sweet was the sound when oft at evening's close
Up yonder hill the village murmur rose,
There as I passed with careless steps and slow
The mingled sounds came softened from below.

Goldsmith

Jessica

I was born in 1923 in Co. Cavan in the Republic of Ireland. We lived on the edge of the Castle Sanderson Estate. My family had been a tenant farmers for four generations. We farmed 45 acres, but now owned it.

My family, the McMahons, as I first recall consisted of Grandad McMahon, Auntie Jeannie, my parents Eleanor and Thomas, three brothers John, Harold and Bob, and my sister Polly.

Our main crops were potatoes and oats and a small quantity of rye. The potatoes and oats formed a large part of our diet. The rye was thrashed carefully by my father and grandad with flails, and the straw was used to thatch our house.

The house was in two parts—the oldest part had a parlour and a dairy downstairs and a large bedroom which held two double beds and a smaller bedroom upstairs. The newer part was just a big kitchen, scullery and a bedroom, and Polly and I had a double bed in the parlour. My parents slept in the bedroom near the kitchen.

My father went out with his gun and shot a few rabbits—not many rabbits died of old age on our farm—and if a pheasant or two flew onto our fields, they didn't always have a return ticket. There was a lough, for some reason called Susie's Lough. My brothers put down set hooks sometimes at night, and we often had a big pike or two, so we ate fairly well.

My mother's family were the Scarletts. They owned their own farm. I don't know how big it was, but there were twelve lovely black and white cows to be milked, night and morning.

My Grandad Scarlett was a cabinet maker, and had a workshop in the barn. His eldest son Robert had worked with him until the war, then had joined the army and come safely through. After that he had opened his own business in Portadown.

My grandmother, Jane Scarlett, and Aunt Anna ran the farm with two farm workers who came in every day.

Uncle Johnny lived there too. He was a horse dealer. He never talked to us children, and he didn't seem to do much work either.

135

When dad was a boy he had worked as a garden boy at the Castle. He started work when he was twelve years old and was there for ten years. By the time he left to marry my mother he was third gardener.

The Sanderson family had left by the time I was born, but there were always stories about them. Colonel Sanderson was a small man, and like many small people he had a big ego. My father said once that when he and grandad were hay-making, there was a thunderstorm brewing and they wanted to get finished before the rain came. The Colonel galloped up on his horse and barked, "There's a fence down in the long meadow—see to it." They had to leave the hay and mend the fence. Dad said he had probably put the horse over it and knocked it down.

Another story, told to me by my uncle Robert: grandad Scarlett was in his workshop when a messenger arrived from the Castle with a note which read, "See me in my office at 10am on Tuesday." Now grandad Scarlett was very much his own man and hated bad manners, so he wrote back, "Dear Sir, I cannot see you in your office on Tuesday, but you can find me in my workshop between the hours of 7.30am and 6pm any day except Sunday. Next morning the Colonel galloped up to the gate. Grandma came out of the house to see what the noise was. He threw her the reins and marched into the workshop. "This is a damned inconvenience, Scarlett." And grandad said, "Good morning, Colonel, How can I help you?" They sorted out what he wanted, and in the meantime grandma had tied the horse to the gate and got on with her work.

I enjoyed going to the Scarletts. Grandma was always cooking—lovely soda bread and home-made jam and nice fruit cakes—and she always let me help.

At mealtimes, grandad got us to talk. He would ask my brothers about school and he made conversation all the time. Afterwards he would show us what he was making in the workshop, and after Sunday dinner we would all walk around the fields and look at the animals. We were always frightened and delighted when he took us to the bull field, where Hector the big black bull puffed and snorted around the gate.

At home, things were very difficult. My grandad McMahon never allowed us to speak at the table. He was a mean little wasp of a man. I never saw him smile, and Aunt Jeannie was the same. She was very pious and was constantly correcting us. When I was about seven or eight years old, I used to answer her back or argue with her if no-one else was about. She was tall and raw-boned—she had long, narrow feet and walked with her feet at ten to two. She had big red hands with knuckles sticking out—she had grey hair which she wore in a bun on top of her head, and as she did a lot of knitting there were usually a couple of knitting needles stuck through the bun.

I remember one Sunday morning, I was singing a song we had learned at school. She grabbed my arm and said, "You don't sing songs on Sunday," and I said, "And you shouldn't sing hymns on Monday." Mum and dad thought it was hilarious, but she was livid and later on, on our way to Sunday school (she was the teacher), she took hold of my hand and dragged me all the two miles to the church—and could she stride out! My hand was white and numb all through Sunday school.

My mother used to tell me about the bad old days, when she and dad had to come back when grandma broke her hip.

My mother was visiting her parents then, and mentioned that she had two broody hens, so when she was leaving to come home grandma gave her twelve goose eggs and told her to slip six under each hen, and she would have a few geese for the Christmas market. So mother did, and said nothing to anyone—and by and by they all hatched out. Mother says she doesn't know who got the greater shock, the mother hens or my grandad, who demanded to know what she thought she was doing. Didn't she know that twelve geese ate as much as a cow and a half? However, she reared them and took them to market, and instead of bringing the money home to grandad she bought a puny pair of turkeys and a little sow.

Grandad nearly had a stroke, but she stood up to him, and her turkeys flourished, and in the spring the hen bird laid twelve eggs and hatched out a nice flock. And the little sow in the fullness of time visited the old boar up the road and had a good litter. So mother was getting things going. That was her favourite saying: "Come on children, let's get things going."

When I was born, Aunt Jeannie told mother I looked like a monkey, black hair, eyes that missed nothing, and a splendid pair of lungs when I needed attention. Can you forgive someone who compared you to a monkey?

Fifth child came fairly low in the pecking order. In fact, looking back, I think the animals and turkeys got more attention than the children. My mother would kneel down and scratch the sow's back for minutes at a time, and feed the little turkeys from her hand to make sure they all got a share. We were washed and fed, and got a smart slap if we misbehaved and a kiss going to bed.

My sister Polly was very pretty—long golden curls to her waist, a skin like peaches and cream, and she was so good—always helping mother and keeping herself clean and tidy. I, on the other hand, couldn't stay clean for more than ten minutes—my hair was black and straight and I was a very ordinary child.

After church on Sunday we would all stand around outside and chat to our neighbours, and the ladies would say, "Hello Polly, aren't you a lovely girl, and a great help to your mother I hear." Then they would notice me. "Hello, and how are you?" Me, I was just fine, not lovely and no help to my mother—that's life.

When Polly caught the mumps I couldn't believe it. There she was, her face all lop-sided and her eyes nearly closed. I just sat staring at her until she started to cry, and mother told me to find something to do. It was the happiest two weeks of my life when Polly had the mumps.

• • •

We had two near neighbours, the Tighes and the Cassidys.

The Tighes were a hard-working family. Mrs Tighe was a widow with a girl and a boy, Cissie and Johnny. They all lived with Mrs Tighe's brother, Tommy Mulligan. Cissie and I have stayed friends, and to this day we keep in touch although we are both in our seventies.

Johnny moved away and married in Sligo. He worked for the Forestry Commission, and had eight children who all did well at school. Cissie never married. She looked after the farm and then nursed first her uncle, and then her mother. They both lived well into their eighties. She then let the land, and went as housekeeper to the parish priest, and she is still working today. She is a good friend—she's a Catholic and I'm a Protestant, and we have never had an angry word.

The Cassidys were a different story. John and Kate were both over thirty when they got married—it was a match marriage, and a bad match. John was quite a mild, loveable man, but he liked to go for a drink on Saturday evening. When his mother was alive she used to make him something special for supper on Saturday night, and he came home, ate his supper and went to bed.

Katie was a terrible cook, and she never had anything in the house for John's supper, so one night he hit her, and she came crying to our house and slept in grandad's chair.

They had two children, Pat and Rosie. Mum felt so sorry for the children—she thought it was awful for them seeing their parents fighting. One Saturday, mum cut up some boiled bacon and a bit of pickle and half a soda cake. She took it over to the Cassidys for John's supper. Hoping for a quiet night we all went to bed, but at 11 o'clock there was a 'bang, bang' on the door and there stood Kate, holding up her very dirty skirt and crying. "He picked me up and threw me into a bed of nettles," she said. "Didn't he want his supper?" mum asked. "Well," sobbed Kate, "the children and I ate it before he got home."

Pat was a very special friend of mine. He was six months older than me, and ate more food in our house than he got at home. We used to wander barefoot around the fields and paddle in the stream. The soil was peat and the water was brown, and our feet under the water turned a lovely amber colour.

There was a meeting place where all the teenagers got together on summer evenings. We, of course, were tucked up in bed when they met, but one day we were at this meeting place and found a cigarette packet with one cigarette left in. We decided we could smoke it if we had a match, so Pat went into the field where his father was working. He knew John always put his pipe and baccy and matches under his jacket near the gate, so he took one match, a red-headed match—I remember it well. When we struck it on a stone it broke and the lighted end fell into a small pile of dry grass, and it lit up. We kept trying to light the fag, but the flame was spreading and we got scared and ran as far and as fast as our legs could take us. There was a little house on the far side of the common, and everyone came to beat out the fire. They managed to keep it away from the house, but then started asking, "How did it start?" All the children were at school—they never thought about us, thank goodness. We were so frightened we never mentioned it again, and it was many years before either of us lit a cigarette again.

On another occasion we were playing in Pat's barn. There was a broody hen sitting on eggs in a box and we thought we would have a look to see how the hatching was going. Somehow we got the hen off the eggs. We cracked one egg and there was this little bald chicken. We tried to feed it, but it wouldn't eat, so we cracked another and another, and then Kate came in and yelled at us. I got out of the way, but she picked up a twig and caught Pat—he had stripes on his legs for a week. I got a few slaps from my mam when Kate told her.

When I was four years old, Pat's old cat had kittens. There were six of them, but I fell in love with a little ginger one. I took it home and mam yelled at me, "Take it back—we've already got a cat."

Some weeks later I saw Daddy harnessing the pony, I called out, "Can I come?"

"Not today pet," he said, "go and find Pat."

I found Pat sitting on the bank at the end of the lane. "Your father's gone off in a hurry," he said.

"I know," I said, "I asked him if I could come, but he said no."

We sat on the grass in our bare feet. Pat picked the daisies around us and I made a daisy chain. Presently Daddy came back, there was a lady with him.

"That's the woman who brings the babies," Pat said.

I felt a bit uneasy. I wondered if Auntie Jeannie had ordered one—it was the kind of thing she would do, just to spite me. I knew Mam didn't want a baby, she said I was as much trouble as ten babies. However some hours later Daddy carried me into the bedroom, and the strange lady was holding the biggest ugliest baby I had ever seen.

Mam said, "Jessie this is your new little brother."

I shouted at the woman, "Take it back, I've already got three brothers, we don't really need him."

However he stayed, unlike the cat. He was my brother Bill—big bossy Bill.

That was a bad year. Apart from having brother Bill, both my grandparents died. I regret that I didn't miss grandad McMahon, but I missed grandad Scarlett—nothing was ever the same again.

My eldest brother John was a quiet person. He was nine years older than I, and could play any musical instrument all by himself given a couple of hours. He was given a violin by a family friend who emigrated to Canada. Someone showed him how to make chords, and he very quickly learned to play. He also played the bagpipes in a band and could play my mother's accordion.

He also had a passion for engines. By playing the violin at dances, he saved up and bought an old motorbike. Most of the time the engine was in pieces on a bit of old sacking. I remember standing watching him mending a puncture, and accidentally stood on the tube of solution in my bare feet. When I tried to run away, my feet were stuck to the sacking and all the nuts and bolts went flying over the yard. What a job I had getting that stuff from between my toes, and I had to move very fast to get away from brother John.

Nothing came easy or could be taken for granted in rural Ireland during the 20's.

In March, whatever the weather, peat was cut. Turf fires and wood were the only way we had to cook our food or warm the house.

The turfs were about 8" by 4" and about 3" deep. They were cut out of the bog and made into little castles so the air could get through to dry them, then they were moved and turned several times during the summer and finally brought into the turf shed and carefully stacked. Our house was lit by paraffin oil lamps and candles, the paraffin coming from a little general store and public house about two miles away.

After school one of us children used to take a dozen eggs in one hand and the oil can in the other. The eggs were usually a shilling per dozen, that bought ½ a gallon of paraffin and an ounce of tobacco for Dad, and that was several times each week.

Another grocer had a horse and big cart and he called every Monday and took what was left of the eggs, and hopefully they would buy the other provisions.

Planting of potatoes: My mother and father prepared the ground and spread the manure, and after school the children dropped the potatoes and the parents covered them, then home to tea and bread and jam for the children; the parents milked the cows and put the turkeys to bed then wearily put us to bed; and I expect they got to bed early too after Mam had washed out our underwear—we only had two sets each so she washed them every night.

Digging the potatoes was the same—they dug all day and we picked them up after school.

The milk went to the creamery, except for Saturdays and Sundays, was churned, and the butter used for our bread and the buttermilk to make soda bread and to feed the calves and pigs.

My mother had some beehives too. The good honey in squares went to market, the rough honey was squeezed out of the comb and was lovely on bread or porridge, and Mam sweetened apple pies with it. She had an old saucepan which she put the honey comb in with some lavender oil and, I think, linseed oil and camphor. She cooked them all up and poured it into old tins to make wonderful furniture polish. Not a bit was wasted in our house; Mam made jams and jellies from black currents and blackberries and crab apples, and we had a lot of plum trees, russets and Bramley apples and two pear trees which Dad had grafted to a couple of blackthorn trees.

We had, when I was small, two cows, Old Bertha the sow, a couple of Nannie goats, a pony which Grandad used to harness to a little trap and drive to church or to town, and an old donkey called Sally. We also had a lovely little cream and white sheepdog called Tess, and a big black cat who seldom came near us, but my father valued him highly as he caught rats and mice and always put them on the door-step. The sheep dog was a natural—she rounded up the two cows and had them waiting at the gate at milking time, and if a few of us children were playing near the house she would round us up too until we called Mam to call her off.

Sally the donkey was harnessed every weekday and took the milk to the creamery, four miles away. One day the creamery manager said to Dad, "Why don't you get a horse and dray and collect the churns from the other farmers on the way? They are wasting half a day and so are you, and I would get done quicker if all the milk was on one cart instead of a dozen or more trying to get in first."

So Dad asked the farmers, and they were delighted. The manager deducted a penny per gallon to pay Dad from their monthly milk cheques, Dad borrowed the money from the bank to buy the horse and Grandad Scarlett made a good strong dray, and for many years this was a good source of income. Later on another horse and dray was needed as more and more of the local farmers saw the benefit of it, so my brother John drove the second dray. Mother decided to keep the little heifer calf which normally was sold, so we now had three cows.

We lived in a mainly catholic area and there were a few families who supported the IRA—they were called the Fenians then. However, I think they thought Dad was getting too big for his boots and one morning he went out to find a shaft cut off each of the drays. So there was a great scurry around, and we went in all directions telling the farmers they would have to manage for a couple of days. But two days later Grandad Scarlett had put a new shaft in each, and Dad and John were back on the road again.

In December 1931 my youngest brother was born. He was small and quite sweet, but I would have liked a little sister. Mam wasn't very well for a while, and the doctor came out to see her for weeks afterwards.

When Marshall (that's what they called him) was three months old, Bill and I caught whooping cough and then the baby got it. Mam was at her wits end—everyone thought the baby would die. Bill and I used to stand clinging to each other and whooping and sometimes we were down on our knees, but we all survived and thanks to Mam's lovely honey and goats milk we are all still alive.

In September 1932, Mother woke suddenly and thought she smelt burning. She got up and woke Dad and picked up the baby, then when she opened the bedroom door the smoke nearly drove her back. She ran and roused us all—the small part of the house was on fire. The big boys roused the neighbours who all helped, and the older part was saved. Apart from water and smoke damage, we could live in it. Sadly it wasn't insured, which was remiss of Mam—she was usually careful about that sort of thing.

We got a grant from the government to rebuild, and it was back in use in about 18 months. Mam and Dad always believed the IRA did it—there was no other reason. The grate was carefully covered with ashes at bed time, and the fire had started over the front door at 3 o'clock in the morning.

My parents never got over the fire. They got up during the night to check everything, and working hard and not getting their sleep took its toll.

Water was another problem. The drinking water was a spring well two fields away. The water for washing, etc., came from a water butt which caught the rain on the galvanised roof of the byre. Hopefully it rained enough for wash day on Monday, otherwise we had to carry the water in buckets from a stream.

John, my brother, later made a little cart with four old pram wheels so one person could carry four buckets-full in one go.

I've got long arms due, I'm sure, to the number of buckets of water I carried from the spring well. It was lovely water, as cold as ice and clear as crystal. There was an old root sticking out above the well, and Mam hung an enamel mug on it so we could have a drink before the journey back. Sometimes the rim of the bucket banged against my ankle bone, and if you chanced to stumble you got a shoe full of water and a ticking off from Mam—she wanted full buckets, not halves.

My brother Harold was my favourite—he was thin and wiry with a head of black curls, lovely clear skin and brilliant blue eyes. He was often in trouble with Dad and he got into the greatest mischief imaginable. He and John went fishing in Susie's Lough, and on the way back they had to cross a stile. Harold was in front and decided to jump it. As he jumped, the fishing line snaked out behind him and caught in John's nose, and Harold led him home crying. Dad had to take him to the Doctors to get the hook out.

Harold always resented having to go to church at 2pm every Sunday—all boys who lived near us were Catholic and went to mass early in the morning, and in the afternoon they were free to go hare coursing or just taking the dogs and chasing rabbits.

One Sunday, Auntie Jeannie was away and Mam and Dad weren't coming to church, so when we set off Harold announced that he wasn't going. He said he would meet us when we came out, and warned us not to tell.

So he met up, and we all came home and sat down to tea. Then Dad suddenly looked across at Harold and said, "What was the text in church today ?"

Harold never turned a hair, and answered, "Behold I wasn't there."

My heart was thumping. I waited for Dad to ask where that text came from, but he just carried on with his tea.

We attended the Catholic school because the Protestant one was four miles away, and far too far for six-year olds to walk. Then a rector from a neighbouring parish came to see us, and said that if we could go to his school he would send a horse and buggy for us. What a buggy! It was like the old covered wagon in the western films, but it took us and picked up other children on the way.

Most of our social life was based around the church—Sunday School, Choir, Harvest Thanksgiving. Ours wasn't a parish church—it was the little Castle Sanderson private church—and we didn't have a vicar, so one was sent from the parishes around.

One preacher comes to mind, the Reverend Doctor Gamble. He was a very big man, a bachelor with beautifully cut suits. He had a big red face, and large, fat, red hands, and a big voice which sounded like it was coming out of a tunnel. Us children were bored to tears with his sermons, which went on a bit, but towards the end when he would say, "Pause brethren, pause," and put his two big hands on the pulpit rail, Harold and I would look at each other and get the giggles.

One Sunday he was speaking about the ten virgins and their lamps, and ended by saying, "Pause brethren, pause—is it not better to be in the light with the wise virgins than be in the dark with the foolish ones?" I was too young to get the joke, but Harold was stuffing his handkerchief into his mouth and I just laughed out loud. Luckily we sat in the back pew as Dad lifted the collection, and he bundled the pair of us out through the belfry doors and said, "Home!"

We hurried home and got the tea ready.

Mam and Dad came in first and didn't say anything, then Aunt Jeannie arrived, glared at us, and walked through and slammed the door.

"What's the matter with her?" John asked—he hadn't been at church.

Dad said with a twinkle in his eyes, "I think she's gone to trim her lamps!"

So John was told the joke, and we got off.

Harvest Thanksgiving was always a great time for us. Dad made little sheaves of oats and rye and tied them crossed on the ends of the pews. Mam made lovely loaves of bread, and there was only what people grew in their gardens or on their land or picked from the hedgerows—no tins of peas and beans like today. The church windows were filled with flowers, and fruit and vegetables piled by the communion rails. The altar window-sill was bedded with moss and had a text written in flowers.

At Christmas we had a party in the old school house, with a large Christmas tree and little real candles and lovely old-fashioned ornaments—quite magic. Each child had a present from the tree. All the adults came, and the women made lovely food, and after we had eaten we pulled crackers, and everyone did their party pieces and got great applause, whether they were good or not. The men kept an eye on the candles, in case of fire, and snuffed them as they burnt out.

If old Bertha the sow had a good litter, one was kept for our own use. It was lovely to have a nice crispy rasher in our school sandwiches.

The oats were thrashed by a farmer who went round the small farms with his threshing machine. All the neighbours came to help, and when it was their turn Dad and the boys went to them. The oats went to the mill, and it was porridge for breakfast for us all and porridge for the little turkeys with chopped nettles added at the last minute. Enough oats were kept back for the horses and the chickens and for next year's seed. I think the rye was ground for animal feed.

My father never lost his love of gardening, and we grew cabbages, carrots, onions, swede, parsnips, lettuce and spring onions; also peas and broad beans; so with rabbit, pheasant, bacon and an occasional pike we lived well, and nobody in the house was over-weight.

My brother Bob, three years older than I, was quite a secretive boy. If the rest of us had sixpence we told the world, but Bob hid his pennies, looked after his clothes and always polished his own shoes. It was a horrible chore every Saturday when one of us (usually me) had to polish all the shoes for Sunday for church.

Bob was like John, very musical. He used to sit in the orchard and play his mouth-organ, and later he somehow managed to buy a saxophone. He learned the notes and practised every chance he got in the bedroom.

He played with a group of lads—one on the violin, one the guitar and one the drums—and later joined a well known band and played on radio several times. He really hated farm work and only did what had to be done. Mam had her work cut out getting him up in the mornings if he'd been out with the band the night before.

My brother Bill was the tough one. He was big and broad and very handsome. He argued with everyone about everything, and had a fight at school almost every day and usually won.

When the opticians visited the school they decided he needed glasses, and he marched off to school wearing his new wire rims. When he came home, one lens was on his forehead and the other down on his cheek. Mam tried to straighten them but they snapped in half at the bridge. He got another pair and they ended up the same way, and finally everyone gave up.

About that time, the covered wagon stopped running and we had to walk all the way to school.

Polly was fourteen and had started working for the Reverend Foster at the Rectory of Drumully Parish. The little parish school was low on pupils and would perhaps have to close, so the Reverend said he would buy Bob, Bill and me second-hand bicycles if we would go to his school. It was about 7 miles morning and afternoon, but we went. It was a nice little school. The teacher, Miss Curry, was about 23 years old, she had BSc after her name, and she was quite strict.

One day at school a boy called Bertie Nesbutt told her that Bill had thrown a dead rat into the school well. I knew at once that Bill wouldn't do this, as he was fussy about food and drink and would upset my mother at teatime by scalding out his own private mug from the boiling kettle before he drank out of it. So Miss Curry called Bill out, got her cane and told him to hold out his hand. He took it from her, broke it in half and handed it back to her.

She said no more then, but the following morning she told the Reverend Foster and he called Bill out. But I came up too, and I told them both that Bertie was a liar, and I took Bill's hand, got our coats and bikes and went home. We told our parents. Bill swore he never did it, and knowing he would need to drink the water himself we believed him. The parents went to the school that afternoon, and next morning nothing was said about it to us.

Bill was also very possessive about his belongings and wouldn't lend a pencil, though he had a pencil-case full, always sharpened. He had a padlock on his bike and on the pump—we could all walk home for all he cared, and we often did, just with a flat tyre.

Another great event on our calendar was the 12th July, in memory of King William's victory over King James at the Battle of the Boyne.

Dad belonged to the Orange Order, a group of staunch Protestant men who had their lodge nights and their secrets, and on the 12th July all the lodges marched at a pre-arranged town. They all had a marching band—flute, silver or brass, with kettle drums and a big drum—and as they marched people stood alongside and cheered them.

I realise now how provocative it was to the Catholics and how dangerous it was for our family coming back late at night, but we all had something new for the 12th and if our neighbour's children weren't so keen to play with us for a few days it was what we expected.

The Catholics had their days too—29th June and 15th August. I don't know what these days were about, but they dressed up and marched and we hadn't anyone to play with then either.

Cissie Tighe was a good friend. She was three years older, but we have stayed friends all our lives. Her uncle Tommy had a great line in ghost stories, and on winter evenings I sometimes went over to Tighes and he would tell us about how, on a summer night with not a breath of air, a bush in our field had been torn out of the ground by the wind, and when he was coming past Cussocks Gate a grey lady was standing there crying. We also got the headless horses rushing up the road at midnight. My parents said don't believe it, but I always hurried past Cussocks Gate just the same. I said to Cissie one day, "I wonder if your Uncle Tommy gets frightened?" and she said, "Oh, take no notice of him, he's such a bloody liar!"

I must mention the saga of the chamber pots. We had no sanitation in those days—the toilet was a little shed with a seat and a bucket under it, well hidden away behind the apple trees. So we had chamber pots under the beds. My mother had a very ornate jug and basin on her wash stand, with this gorgeous pot to match, so pretty it was a shame to pee in it. The rest of us had enamel pots, and they all had to be emptied each day. At first it was Polly's job, and when she left home it was my job. There was a big white slop pail with a lid which we took upstairs, emptying the chamber pots into it, but on Saturday all the pots came down and were scrubbed with Vim and rinsed with Jeyes fluid.

One day I took the pail upstairs, and thought of my book under the mattress—so I lay down on the bed, and you know how time goes, when suddenly Mam called up, "Jessica, have you done the pots?" I dashed into the boys room and did theirs and hurried down and did Mam's, and a while later I remembered my own. I couldn't carry the pot down or the pail up, so I opened the window and tipped it out.

Sadly, Daddy was mending something under the window and caught the lot—he was soaked! I did suffer for that little error, I can tell you!

I often got into trouble for reading when I should have been working.

One November when I was twelve, and the turkeys were nearly ready for market, they were shut in a small field and hadn't much room. Mam liked them to have a run and a good flap in the big field, but someone had to watch them as the fields led into the woods and we had foxes and stray dogs. So I was given the job of looking after them. I put my coat on with my book tucked inside, sat down on an old calf shelter, and, as I said, where does time go when you have a good book?

Suddenly there was a great uproar among the turkeys. They were on the edge of the wood and a great red fox was dragging one into the trees. The rest of the family heard the noise as well, and Mam and Dad came running out. We didn't get that turkey back, but we rounded up the rest and put them safe. Mother broke a strong twig off the lilac bush, grabbed me by my long plait of hair in one hand and I thought she would never stop hitting me with the other.

A few weeks later she and Dad took the turkeys to market. I had decided that my plait of hair would have to go. So after they left I tried to hack it off with the scissors, but Bill and Marshall got my Dad's cut throat razor and they snecked it off. I had forgotten all about it as I stood at the door waiting for them to come back from market.

My mother looked at me and said, "What in God's name have you done now!" She picked up the plait, which was still on the floor, and she tied a ribbon on it and put it away. I thought at the time, that's the first ribbon it's had for a long time. I always lost my ribbons, my hair being so straight. Polly never lost ribbons—she had a bow at the back of her head and it stayed all day. I had an old shoe lace on the end of my plait and I never lost it!

In 1935 a letter came from the Sandersons—did my father have any sons who would like to work in England?

John was gone like a shot, and a month later Harold followed him. Bob took over the creamery cart with my father, but there was no one to do the farming, so the parents decided to sell off the stock and just keep one cow for our own use. Dad let the fields out to another farmer and then, the final straw, a young catholic man bought a lorry. He called on all my father's customers, offered a better price, and the horses and drays became redundant as well. We lived, or should I say existed, on the money from letting the fields—we didn't have many luxuries.

In 1937, the last day of June, the last day at school, there were prizes for good work and good attendance and I got the Bishop's medal for R.E.—and surprise, surprise, I got a little silver cup for the best book of essays.

Miss Curry said, "Keep writing Jessie," and I wondered what on earth was there to write about. A job had been found for me—I would be trained to be a parlour maid, with two cotton dresses for morning and a navy one for afternoons, two pairs of black stockings and a good sensible pair of black shoes.

The Reverend Foster's wife had a cousin, Colonel Marcus Clements, who lived with his wife a two children at Ashfield Lodge. Their Parlour maid was seventy and unwell, and I was going to replace her. I was going to get £1. 6. 8d per month.

How little they knew me. I danced attendance on no-one; I would help a child or an old person, but at fourteen years old I thought that healthy adults should look after themselves.

I packed my few clothes in a little old case—the Fosters came in their car, tied my bicycle on the back and put me and my pathetic little case into the back seat.

Ashfield lodge was about 20 miles away, and we seemed to be going uphill all the way. Mrs Foster was telling me to behave and to do as I was told. I had had the same talk from my mother before I left, and tried to get the 'yes's' and 'no's' in the right places—but I just knew I was going to hate it.

At last we turned into a long drive, over a bridge over the River Ash, and arrived at the front door. It was a long low house in grey stone, with a lovely green lawn and a rose garden. I was sent round the back with my case in one hand and my bike in the other.

I walked through a big yard with lots of buildings and finally found the back door. It was opened by a freckled-faced girl who smiled and said she was Moya the kitchen maid—I was to share a room with her. She took me upstairs and helped me unpack, which took only five minutes, and then we went down to the servants' hall for tea.

I met the Cook, Mrs McKenna, Maud the house maid, Alice the nursery maid and Bob the chauffeur. Bob lived in the rooms over the garage, but ate with us. It was bread and jam, and I thought neither was as good as Mam's; the bread was quite stale. I was told I didn't have to work that day, but when old Sarah came down to do the dining room for dinner I helped her lay up and washed up for her afterwards. She looked so old and frail. After that, she, Cook and I sat down in the servants' hall, and at 9.30 they went to bed. All the girls had disappeared—I went to our bedroom, got into bed and I cried. I wanted my Mam. I couldn't understand myself—I sometimes didn't even like my Mam.

Moya came in at 10 o'clock. "Have you been crying?" she said. "Don't worry, you'll be alright—you can come out with us tomorrow night."

At half past six the next morning, Cook called us and we got up and dressed. Sarah was waiting for me. I had to clean out the ashes in the fireplaces in the dining-room, drawing room and the library. I had to light the dining-room and the library fires, and the drawing room fire was to be lit just before lunch.

On hands and knees I had to brush the carpets in the three rooms and dust them, lay the table for the Colonel's breakfast, sweep the doorstep and the front hall. All this to do before 8.30, and not even a cup of tea.

After serving breakfast we had our own, then checked the dining room, washed up, had twenty minutes to make our own beds, cleaned the silver and the brass cans used for hot water to the bedrooms, and layed up the dining room for lunch. We had our lunch at 12.30—stew, cabbage and potatoes, and rice pudding—every day except Sunday. Roast lunch on Sunday.

Then after cleaning, and washing up the lunch, at about 2.30 Maud and I had to mend the Colonel's socks and underwear, sheets and pillow cases. At 4 o'clock, tea was served in the dining room. At 5 o'clock we had our tea of bread and jam. We had a little time between six and seven, then we layed up for the dinner—4 courses, this meal—then washed up, and about 9 o'clock we were finished. I was almost too tired to go out, but Moya said, "Come on," so I went. Maud disappeared—I found out later she went up to Bob's room over the garage. I hoped she wasn't doing what I thought she was doing up there.

Alice, Moya and I walked down to the bridge, where there were several boys—Alice walked off with a ginger-haired one called George—Moya and I stood talking to the others. One of them I had seen in the morning, watering the flowers in the hall—he was the youngest of three gardeners. He walked back with Moya and me, and next morning at 7am he kissed my cheek in the hall. I was in seventh heaven—I had a boyfriend!

Colonel Clements was probably nearly sixty. He was very ugly with a huge red nose, and wore a wig. It was brown, and I thought if it had been grey he would have looked better. He never spoke to me all the time I was there—I don't think he even saw me. Mrs Clements was about thirty. She walked rather stiffly on a stick. She had a long face, hardly ever smiled, straight brown hair bobbed around and a grip stuck in the side. She wore thick tweed skirts and jumpers, thick stockings and brown brogue shoes.

The children were young—Marcus was three and Catherine about 9 months—and they were pretty. Alice took Marcus out for a walk every morning, and Catherine's pram was outside the pantry window. The Colonel used to walk past the pram, but he never spoke to her or looked at her. I stole out one day and played peep with her around the pram hood, but Nannie caught me and sent me in and told me to get on to my work. Everyone I knew played with babies, but no-one played with little Catherine.

Most of the orders came from Nannie O'Brien. Cook took her book up at 10 o'clock each morning, and Madam ordered the food for the day.

I was very relieved when Nannie told me I needn't light the dining room and library fires as the weather was warmer. I found lighting the fires hard work as the kindling wood was often damp. So my life was easier for a few months. But in the afternoons, when Maud and I were sitting mending, the drawing room bell would ring and Madam would say, "Make up the fire." The logs and coal were beside her. I thought she could have done it herself, but I suppose that was what I was there for.

They didn't entertain very much. Once in a while someone came for afternoon tea, but then I was told that Madam's mother and two brothers were coming to stay for a while.

Her mother looked like Barbara Cartland—perhaps not so much make-up, but very pink, white and fluffy. The eldest brother, Edward, was about 35, had a plummy voice and never spoke to the servants, but Lawrence, the younger one, was just the opposite. He spent more time in the servants' hall than with his family, and used to sit on the pantry shelf while I washed up or cleaned the silver, talking about everything.

Maud's mother died, and she had to go home for the funeral, so I had to take up the early morning tea trays. I was told to knock and when they said, "Come in," I was to put the tray down on the bedside table, draw the curtains, then come out and close the door. Well I knocked, and I thought I heard a voice, so I opened the door. Next to Madam's dark hair was the Colonel's very large bald head, so I quickly backed out and shut the door quietly and knocked again. This time after a few seconds I heard, "Come in." This time the colonel had his wig on.

Lawrence was sitting in the pantry and I told him. He laughed and said, "Do you know, the morning after they got married my sister woke up first and looked at him and said, 'Marcus, darling, your arse is on the pillow.'" I didn't believe it, but he swore it was true. Lawrence also often wore odd socks. I told him once, and he said, "There's a pair the same as this in the drawer."

After dinner, I had to carry the coffee tray around the drawing room. It was solid silver, very heavy, a silver coffee pot and a silver jug with hot milk plus the priceless coffee cups and saucers. I would have loved to drop the lot on the priceless carpet, but as breakages were deducted from our pay, I wisely decided to struggle on.

One evening when I was going around with my tray, Lawrence was sitting in the bay window. I happened to look at him, and he winked—so, fool that I was, I winked back—but Madam's black eyes had seen. Next morning she sent for me. I stood like a criminal before a judge. She sat in her four-poster among the lacy pillows and gave me hell. How dare I look at anyone—you keep your eyes cast down when you are serving—one more incident like that and I would be sent home to my mother.

I think Lawrence got told off too. He told me he was sorry—he hadn't meant to get me into trouble. He said he was bored with his family and was joining a ship at Southampton in two weeks time. I said, "You must be rich to go on a cruise," and he replied, "I'm only paying my fare to Southampton—I'll be working on the ship." "What doing?" I asked. "The same as you are doing," he said, "looking after boring people with too much money." "Well," I said, "don't wink at the ladies or you'll be sent back home to your mother."

I was sad when he left—he was so nice to everyone.

I had every second Sunday off after the lunch, and I rode my bike home, had my tea with my family and rode back. I gave my mother £1 every month, and the 6/8d I spent on having my hair cut, toothpaste, soap and stockings and sometimes I had enough left for a packet of sweets.

After our hour out each night, we girls were hungry—bread and jam at 5 o'clock was a long time ago. One night I had a pain I was so hungry, and the kitchen was all locked up as was the larder. So I said to the others, "I wonder if the pantry keys would fit the kitchen?" I tried and they did. The cupboards were locked too, but again we found a key to open one, and there were cake tins in there. So we got them out, cut a good slice each, then put them away and locked up again.

Next morning Cook was in a right bad mood. She slapped the breakfast dishes on the tray and glared at me. Moya was faring no better, and Alice got shouted at when she came to pick up the nursery tray. Cook took her book up to Madam's room at 10 o'clock and when she came down she told us we had to go to Madam's room at once. She had a nasty glint in her eye and I thought, "Here comes trouble."

There we stood, the four of us, in our print dresses, mop caps and long white aprons and she sat propped up among the pillows. I wanted to laugh but I knew this was serious.

She began: —"Cook tells me the kitchen cupboards were broken into last night, so what have you all got to say?"

I glanced at Moya. She was frightened, so I said, "We didn't break into anything, the pantry keys opened the doors."

"But why did you steal the cakes?"

"We were hungry," I said.

"Hungry?" she said. "Didn't you have your tea at 5 o'clock?"

"We have bread and jam," I said. "The bread is usually stale and we are always hungry at night."

She looked puzzled and then said, "This must never happen again—I will talk to Cook."

We all said sorry and she let us go. We couldn't believe our luck, and at tea time that day we found salad and corned beef, fresh bread and butter and jam.

Cook was like a demon—she actually hit Moya for forgetting something—but when we came in that night there was a plate of sandwiches and a glass of milk each waiting for us in the servants' hall.

Almost a week later it was Nannie who called us at 6.30 in the morning.

Moya said, "Where's Cook?" and Nannie said, "You will have to prepare breakfast on your own—Jessica can help you."

"Is Cook ill?" Moya asked.

"I will talk to you later," Nannie said.

About 9.30 Cook came down carrying her case. She didn't speak to anyone and Bob took her away in the car. We didn't know what to think, but Nannie told Alice that she and Madam had been wondering where all the food was going, so Nannie hid in a corner near the back door. There was a knock and Cook handed the person a bag and said, "There's only eggs and butter in there, them young trollops have been complaining about the food and Madam's on the war path." But Nannie showed herself and took Cook into the Drawing Room. When the Colonel heard all, he gave her instant dismissal and what money she was owed.

So poor Cook shot herself in the foot—she could have gone on feeding her family well on food, if she had kept quiet about the cakes. There's a moral in there somewhere.

Later in the morning Bob went off in the car and came back with an elderly lady. She told us her name was Ellen and that she had been cook at Lough Ryhm for thirty years. Lough Ryhm belonged to another branch of the Clement family. She had retired six months ago and lived with her sister in an estate cottage. She said she hoped to train Moya and hoped we would all be happy together.

I liked her right away. She was cheerful and a brilliant cook, though modest about it. Even the cabbage was green and delicious. She didn't mind me watching her working and told me I would be a better cook than a parlour maid, but I'd have to be a kitchen maid first. I said, "I wouldn't like washing the saucepans," and she said, "I think you're a bit of a handful!"

We were all sorry when she left. Moya was quite a good cook, and we all helped one another, but we used to play terrible tricks on each other too. One day I flicked a bit of whipped cream at Moya and she tipped the whole bowl-full over me. We had to run to the dairymaid for more. She grumbled, but I said I'd stood under the shelf and the bowl had fallen on me.

We soft-soaped Willie Daly too, and got extra fruit from the garden and had late night feasts.

When the war started we were brought into the Drawing Room to hear Chamberlain's speech, and heard him say, "Britain is now at war with Germany."

Madam sat sobbing. I didn't understand why at the time—it was all happening in England and we were in Ireland. But then Mam wrote and said Harold had joined the RAF, but John had been turned down for medical reasons. I wondered if he was ill, but he had a bent toe on each foot and walked badly.

I was getting a bit discontented at Ashfield. I never got used to waiting at table, and I had an insane desire to pour hot soup over the

Colonel's wig. I wanted to do this so badly I was afraid to walk behind his chair with anything in my hand.

Then I got a letter from Aunt Muriel in Belfast, who told me all the girls were flocking to the munitions factories, the boys and men to Harland and Wolfe's, the shipyard, and Short and Harland's, the plane factory. There was plenty of work in Belfast she said, "Why don't you come and live with us and find a job."

So I gave a month's notice and came home for a week. My parents were cross with me for leaving—"You had a job for life there," Mam said. I couldn't believe my ears. Where was the Mam who said, "Come on children, let's get things moving"? This little worried-looking person wasn't the old Mam at all. I told them I would send home money and that I'd get a job in no time at all.

In Belfast I found I needed a Residence Permit, as the Republic of Ireland hadn't joined in the war and I was regarded as alien. I wasn't allowed to work in munitions, but got work in a chain store selling grocery and veg.

The Americans were stationed near Belfast, and we were never short of boyfriends. Betty Hall and I ran the greengrocery branch in Donegal Pass. We had late nights dancing, and a mad rush to catch the bus to work. I was really enjoying myself.

Two young Americans who used to come into the shop asked Betty and me to go to the theatre with them. We decided to go, and agreed that we would stay together and not pair off. We were a bit nervous of these strangers. They reserved seats for us all, and we enjoyed the drama. When we came out, it was summertime and still light. We walked four abreast, and Betty and I wondered why people were turning and looking at us and smiling. It was only when Betty and John moved in front that we found the 'reserved' tickets stuck to her back and mine. They were a lot of fun those two, but they moved on, we weren't allowed to know where.

About a year later I was put in charge of the Lisburn Road branch. My pay had gone up and I sent quite a bit to Mam. She didn't always answer my letters—I was a bit hurt about that.

I joined a cycling club, and at week-ends we would ride out to Bangor and Hollywood, both lovely little seaside towns. We took sandwiches and drinks and we would all sprawl on the grassy banks above the sea and talk, sometimes serious and sometimes just nonsense.

My greatest memory is of VE day; everyone in Belfast seemed to be around the City Hall, and everyone kissed everyone else. Sailors,

Soldiers, Airmen, Policemen, everyone seemed to be off-duty. There were bands playing and singing, and a ring of people holding hands all round the Hall and sang Auld Lang Syne.

Four of us walked back after midnight through the side streets. We stopped at the bonfires—every street had one—and shared roast potatoes baked in the embers, and I arrived back at Auntie Muriel's at 4 am. She was up, and grinned at me and said, "You're early." She made tea and I told her what the city centre was like. She said, "Aren't we lucky that Harold and Tom are safe." Tom was here eldest son, a rear gunner in the RAF; Harold, my brother was in Ceylon. Then we talked about the boys who hadn't come back—so many—and we sat and cried for them, and then I went and had a bath and some breakfast and went to work. It wasn't busy—everyone must have slept until the afternoon.

At the end of 1945 I got a letter to say that my Residence Permit wouldn't be renewed. I was horrified—what had I done wrong? I had stayed with the same firm for four years, I was sober and hardworking. I went down to the local office and asked why. A kindly man explained that when the munitions factories closed there would be a lot of people unemployed, and the same in the shipyards and Short and Harland's. The country was up to its eyes in debt and they couldn't pay dole money to some whilst aliens were earning. I saw the point.

"What about the hospitals?" I asked. Well, he said, not many of the girls wanted to train as nurses—they had got used to big pay packets. A trainee nurse earned very little—but if successful in getting into a hospital to train, they would guarantee the permit until the training was done. Of course if I got into trouble, the permit would end.

I arranged for an interview with the matron of The Royal Victoria Hospital, which was the biggest in the city. She gave me a good grilling, I filled in the application form, went for a medical and passed—I was in good health.

I was to start work on January 1st 1946, and in the meantime I went home and saw my family. I was shocked when I saw my father—he was thin, yellow and walking on sticks. Mam had aged too. I hadn't seen them for two years, which was careless of me, and I felt I ought to stay and help, but Mam said, "We have enough mouths to feed as it is—go back to Belfast and do whatever it is you are doing. Bill and Marshall are here and they can find casual work." Bob had left home when the creamery carts had stopped. "You wouldn't be able to earn a penny here," she told me.

So I started at the hospital, and if I ever had any illusions about the glamorous life of a nurse, I was soon put right. Bring in the bed pans, empty them, change yet another wet and very often dirty bed, empty the spit mugs—that was the worst. I put them on a tray, put a cloth over them, carried them to the sluice, closed my eyes, took the cover off and turned the taps on full. I didn't open my eyes until I was sure they were clean.

There were seven new recruits. We all slept on the same floor, and we learned how to make beds, lift patients, take round meals, and feed the helpless. Sister Turner was strict but fair, and would throw in a word of praise now and then.

On April 1st we had an exam—the three months were only a trial. I had no trouble with the written paper, but in the practical I nearly lost my nerve and made a few mistakes—but I got through—the real training had started.

I was on the male ward. Many of the patients were soldiers back from France, some whose nerves were in shreds, some without an arm or leg or both. I used to tell them jokes, dirty and otherwise—I loved to make them laugh. One or two proposed to me and I promised to think about it.

At the end of May I had a letter from Mam. Dad had cancer, I'd have to come home and help her. I saw matron and showed her the letter—she wasn't best pleased. She pointed out how much trouble they had gone to get me this far, and finally said if I was back in six weeks I could carry on, but any longer than that and she couldn't help me. But it took six painful months for Dad to die, and by that time I'd had enough nursing to last me a lifetime.

The day after the funeral, Mother told me to find a job. I hadn't had a full night's sleep for six months, but I had to move on. Mother didn't look well, and she hadn't cried or shown any emotion at all. I wanted to stay and look after her and the boys, but she wouldn't have it—she said life had to go on.

I had been thinking about coming over to England. I wrote to my brother John and he said, come over anyway, you will soon find something.

I heard that a couple in our local town wanted help with two small children. I needed the money for my fare , so I worked there until February, also giving my mother a little money—she grumbled a bit, but I did scrape together £20 and caught the night boat from Belfast to Heysham.

It was a terrible winter that year, 1946–1947—the snow froze on top of snow, and the trees were encased in ice. John met me a Euston. We hadn't seen each other for twelve years. He looked the same, but he didn't recognise me. I'd bought some good clothes when I worked in Belfast—Aunt Anna used to send me her clothing coupons and I paid for quality stuff, going to Robinson and Cleavers, the best store in Belfast. I had two good suits and a lovely camel hair coat as well as lots of skirts and dresses.

John's wife had expected a shabby little country mouse, and she took an instant dislike to me. I tried to be nice to them all, but I was glad when I got a job at Well Manor Farm. It was owned by Major Hope and Major Hesletine. Major Hope was married to a lovely lady called Grace, and they had a little girl. I was just a general help, and I could cook quite well—I had learned a lot at Ashfield Lodge. There was a land girl there too called Jean—I think she had designs on Major Hesletine who was a bachelor. One Sunday he asked me to come round the farm with him—I really enjoyed that walk. I told him about our little farm, and he was a good listener and told me their plans. When we got back Jean was very cross—she watched me all the time.

We used to go across the road to a little old pub—*The Chequers*—which was owned by a dear old man called Mr Bundy. He used to be the Headley policeman, and he told me many stories about the village and the bad boys there—in those days he used to box their ears and send them home.

My brother John and his family lived at *Oaks* in Headley—in the cottage. Violet, his wife, cooked for Mrs Townley-Parker and there was a daily help who came in to do the cleaning. Then the daily left, and Violet decided it would be a good idea if I came and lived in at *Oaks* and did the cleaning. It wasn't a wise move on my part. I was a cheap baby-sitter, until I met Percy Woodger, and he and I went out about three or four times each week.

Finally John and his family moved out—they never stayed very long anywhere. Mrs Townley-Parker decided to go abroad for the winter—I couldn't stay alone in the house, so Percy and I decided to get married.

In February 1948 my mother died. I couldn't get home in time for the funeral—in Ireland funerals are two days after a death. I had to go by train, boat and train, and I got there the day after. The house was in a terrible state. Mother had died of a brain tumour and she hadn't done any cleaning for months. Bill and Marshall were there, and there was no food in the house—Bill was 19 and Marshall was 15. I gave them some money to go and buy some food—I didn't know where I was going to sleep, as there wasn't a clean sheet in the place, but Cissie Tighe came over and told me I could sleep at their house. I did what I could for the boys and brought Marshall back to England with me. I didn't know what to do with him when we got there, but Cissie's mother said if he stayed in Ireland he would end up in prison. I had just enough money to get us to Haslemere Station—we hadn't had anything to eat for 24 hours, only water. John met us—he had a taxi, and took Marshall home with him. Violet didn't like Marshall either and he was very unhappy—he had just lost his Mam and was in a strange country. He got a job at first in Headley working at the Land of Nod, but then Mrs Townley-Parker got him into a hostel in London. There he worked in the Palm Toffee Factory, and when he turned eighteen he was called up for National Service.

Percy and I got married in June 1948. We lived in the Oaks Cottage until Christmas that year. I was pregnant and Mrs Townley-Parker was due back. I knew she didn't care for children, and I knew we wouldn't get Council accommodation while we lived there, so we moved in with Percy's Auntie Lil at Fairview Terrace. We had the tiny back bedroom and the front room downstairs.

Lil had five children and was divorced from her husband, but we got on very well with each other. There were six houses in the terrace, and all except one was occupied by Percy's family. They often fell out and there were terrible rows—there was never a time when they were all speaking to each other, and when they quarrelled the language was very colourful to say the least.

Our son Robin was born while we lived there, and just before Irene was born fifteen months later we were given a house at Erie Camp, which had been a Canadian military camp during the war. It wasn't a palace by any stretch of the imagination, but we had three bedrooms, a large kitchen and a bathroom.

The day before we left, Lil and Mother-in-law had a real fight, and ma-in-law threw the slop bucket over her. I felt sorry for Lil with no man to back her up, but I've got to say she could hold her own, and I almost enjoyed that fight, knowing I only had one more night to spend there.

We scoured the local papers for furniture, and for fifteen pounds we got a table, four chairs, a nice little single bed and a terrible double bed—it had a horsehair mattress over a wire base, and when we got into bed we both dropped into the middle. We could never stay bad friends in that bed—in fact I could say it saved the marriage.

Irene was born in May that year, 1950. Judy was born in 1952, and Penny three years later in 1955. Sadly, Penny was mentally handicapped. By the time Penny was two I was very depressed. My doctor told me to find a little evening job, "Just something to get you out." My husband wasn't too happy.

"Who's going to look after Penny?" he demanded.

"You are," I told him.

"I'm tired when I get home," he protested.

"So am I," I snapped, "and I'm tired of washing and ironing and cooking and shopping and picking up and cleaning behind you all and looking after Penny all day and all night."

I found a little job waiting at table at Lloyds Bank Training Centre three evenings a week, and I loved it.

When Penny was four, she started at the Training Centre in Aldershot, and I was offered a job cooking in the kitchen from ten till two. I found a champion in the old chef. Go to Technical College, he advised, learn the trade properly and you will never have to wash another pot.

So I set the family down around the table. The children were very supportive, offering to look after Penny and do the washing up. I said it was only one evening, Wednesday I think.

"Well that's out," Percy said, "Wednesday is my darts night."

"I'll be home by eight thirty," I said.

"And what about the evening meal?"

"It will be in the oven ready to dish up."

"Well, I don't like it at all," he shouted, and slammed out of the house, first to Mammy and then to the pub.

I thought, 'I prayed to God for help, Percy prayed to his mother'— he usually got better results than I did.

Next day I had a visit from ma-in-law. She lost no time in telling me how selfish I was being. I had a good husband, she told me, and looking after the house was my job—men needed their rest. I listened for a while and then I said how would he manage if I packed my case and left for good, and then I lost my cool completely and called her an interfering old bag, and told her to go home and take Percy with her.

After she had gone, I stood shivering. What had I done? Percy would kill me. But he was as good as gold, and when I met Lil at the shop, she laughed and said, "What on earth did you say to Daisy?— she's been as quiet as a mouse."

"I just asked her to mind her own business," I said.

160

On Saturday she turned up with a bag of vegetables as though nothing had happened, and we never had another cross word.

So I did four years at Guildford Tech, passed my exam, and went to cook for the Army. I learned a lot there, and stayed until 1962. I then went as supervisor to Mill Chase School at Bordon and stayed there until 1970.

Penny was sixteen the next year, and was taken into care. Rene got married in February 1972, Judy got married in September the same year, and I became catering manager at King George's Hospital at Liphook. I also looked after the catering at Petersfield Hospital, Heathside Hospital, The Grange Nursing Home, and Wenhem Holt Nursing Home, where I stayed until I retired in 1983.

With Penny in care and the others married, I was able to take a holiday every year. Percy would never come. I think his years in the Navy during the war had been a bad experience for him—he never left home and never wanted to.

I went to Ireland and stayed with my sister Polly—she'd married John Phain in 1942, and they had two lovely sons, Ken and David. Ken married in 1972 and David in 1978. Sadly Polly died in 1988 and I went over to Ireland and stayed with her during her short illness. Poor John was heart-broken—they had had a good solid marriage and I wondered how he would manage, but I was surprised to find him looking after himself very well when I went to stay the following year. John and I always got on very well and I enjoyed his company.

In 1990 I was going over again and my son Robin said he would love to come too. His wife Eileen didn't fancy it—there was a lot of trouble, bombs and shooting—and she said Robin was welcome to go, so he and I flew over from Heathrow. We hired a car for the week— he wanted to see the old homestead, the church and school I had attended and meet Pat Cassidy and Cissie Tighe, my oldest friends.

On Sunday we drove up from Maguires Bridge to Cavan and called in to see an ancient couple, Mary Ann and Frank McKennan— she was 98 and he was 97, but they both recognised me and were very bright and alert.

I asked Robin to stop the car at Wattlebridge. Leaning on the bridge I showed him the Castle, and it was lovely—the undergrowth had all been cut back and the castle stood there reflected in the river. We drove on and I said we will soon see the Fermanagh Gates—what met our eyes was indeed the beautiful old gates, but the spiked fence on one side had been taken away and a petrol station and supermarket built, and there was a queue of cars waiting for petrol as far as one could see. I couldn't believe my eyes.

We carried on until we came to what used to be Reilly's pub and general store—it too had gone, and a beautiful chalet-type building stood back from the road with Legakelly Inn over the door. We decided to go in—there were a few people sitting, so we ordered coffee and sandwiches. A young girl served us, but an older man behind the bar seemed familiar. I went and spoke to him—it was Jim Farley, a boy I had been to school with. He didn't recognise me, but he told me the old pub was bombed and Bertie Reilly had moved away. He and his brother had bought it and built the new one, and were able to make a living. It was very smart—green velvet chairs and seats around little round tables, and the toilets were very clean and well decorated. There were flowers and plants everywhere—I was impressed. I asked him about the queue of cars, and he said the petrol was about half the price in Fermanagh so people came and filled up on Sunday. He said they queued all day Saturday and Sunday until it ran out.

I was dreading the next step of our journey, which was to my old home. I had seen it from the road, but Robin wanted to prowl around and he wanted me to tell him about it, so we parked the car on the roadside and fought our way through weeds and brambles in the lane. My father's lovely thorn hedges, clipped to perfection in my childhood, grew bent and straddled the lane. There wasn't much left of the house, and the old part which was thatched was just a pile of rubble. The part which had been burnt had been tiled, and some of it stood. Robin picked his way through it all and I stood and wept. He took photos and at last picked up a stone and carried it back to the car. "I will put it in my garden," he said.

We called in to see Pat Cassidy—he now had a smart bungalow where the old cottage used to be. He had married Bridie and they had seven or eight children, all now grown and gone. We talked of old times and Pat said, "Do you remember when your father used to take us through the wild garden?" I asked who looked after it now. He turned to me and said that they'd bulldozed it in the 50s. I stared in horror. "All those lovely trees and shrubs?" "Yes," he said, "and they filled in the lake."

That was the final straw—I vowed never to go back there again. A little community had died and only Pat and Bridie, the poorest of us all, are still there—growing old, like I am—but I wonder, if we had all stayed, how would we have fared?

And now ...

꧁ ꧁ ꧁

Oft in the stilly night,
Ere slumbers' chains have bound me,
Fond memories bring the light
Of other days around me.

And now ...

When Percy and I got married in 1948, the wise old villagers shook their heads and said, "It won't last," or "I give them six months."

And, you know, they were almost right. I was 25 and Percy was 26, and neither of us had a clue about managing money or living on a working man's wage.

I was quite a good cook, but I had never had to buy food, and Percy had just come out of the Navy and was still living it up on his gratuity, which had just run out by the time we reached the altar.

We were a right pair of greenhorns. He earned four pounds and ten shillings per week—he gave me two pounds ten shillings and kept two pounds for his beer and cigarettes. He got paid on Friday, and by Tuesday I had no money left, and neither had he.

After Robin was born, I used to push the pram down to the fields and pick peas, strawberries or potatoes, and—God (and Peter Ellis!) forgive me—I often put a few new potatoes in the bottom of the pram.

But by the time our fourth child was born, we had at last learned to live on our income, though nothing grand. Mind you, there were a few battles—nothing physical, just great arguments.

And we must have loved each other, because we stayed together until his sudden death in 1991—that was a great shock after forty-three years.

So now, here in Headley, I am surrounded by love from my four children, eight grandchildren, and seven great-grandchildren (and at the time of writing, three more on the way).

I am well looked after, and happy living alone with my cat Leo.

Long may it continue.

Also by Jessie Woodger

CONNOLLY'S PASS

When, as a young girl, the author wanted to have an excuse to give to her mother when she came home from her ramblings, she would tell her, "I've just been over to Connolly's."
The Connollys didn't exist—they were an invention of young Jessica's fertile imagination. So, when she came to write her first novel, what better than to make them come to life?

• • •

In the book, we follow the story of Rosie Connolly. After the tragic death of her husband, she sets about raising her six children in a small Irish village, with her pride in their achievements overshadowed only by the involvement of one of them in the Provisional IRA.

This heart-warming story is told with great charm, and vividly captures the conventions and beliefs of a closely-knit rural community.

Published by Janus Publishing Company
ISBN 1-85756-306-9